Praise for *Bec*

"After decades of Stephen Levine['s] vice, who better to bring us the st[ory] [of] [t]ransformative journey of Miao Shan becoming Kuan Yin, the Bodhisattva of Compassion."
—Ram Dass, author of *Be Here Now*

"Compassion is the root of healing. It's the doorway to the real miracle, which is an open heart. In this most extraordinary book, Stephen Levine shows us why, and how. Highly recommended."
—Dean Ornish, M.D., Founder and President,
Preventive Medicine Research Institute
Clinical Professor of Medicine, University of California,
San Francisco, author of *The Spectrum* and *Dr. Dean Ornish's
Program for Reversing Heart Disease*

"A loving poetic fable, filled with the mercy of Kuan Yin and the devotion to love that is Stephen and Ondrea's life work and gift to the world."
—Jack Kornfield, author of *A Path with Heart*

"Becoming Kuan Yin is our true work—mine, yours—and a marvelous path from the head to the heart, right into the splendid universe of her Buddha heartsoul. I bow and reverence the radiant Buddha within our own innate original goodness; don't overlook her! Unconditional Compassion is the way, the truth, and the light, and Stephen's long awaited guide takes us right in. Meet ya there!"
—Lama Surya Das, author of *Awakening the Buddha Within*

"The stories of Kuan Yin here are truly captivating and liberating. Through these stories and his own insights, Stephen Levine encourages us to cultivate our own limitless capacity for love and compassion."
—Sharon Salzberg, author of *Real Happiness*

"This book expanded our experience with Kuan Yin to a new level beyond our imagination. This is truly a Masterful book that most assuredly will become a classic. In a very real sense, it felt to us that this book was written at the Gates to Heaven. We found no separation between Kuan Yin's commitment to her Spiritual Life and Stephen's and Ondrea's commitment to their spiritual life and journey. The Levines, in almost a magical way, make Kuan Yin and her life of Compassion, Loving Kindness, and Charity very much alive in every reader's mind."

—Gerald Jampolsky, M.D. and
Diane Cirincione-Jampolsky, Ph.D.

"Stephen's transformational book about the life, teachings, and example of Kuan Yin has the rare power to change people's lives by shifting their reality. For months I have been enduring severe nerve pain, yet it wasn't until I read Stephen's book, *Becoming Kuan Yin: The Evolution of Compassion*, that my heart fully opened to practicing a profoundly merciful, and compassionate approach to my pain."

—Susan S. Trout, Ph.D., co-founder and President of the
Institute for the Advancement of Service, Alexandria, VA

"Stephen Levine's new book, *Becoming Kuan Yin*, is a beautifully written masterpiece that embraces the reader in a reverent flow. The tale of awakening, alternating with principles of practice and guided meditations, opens the heart and generates a profound inner stillness. A remarkable and vibrant transmission of love."

—Francine Shapiro, Ph.D., originator of EMDR therapy,
author of *Getting Past Your Past*

"Good news: the cosmos is compassionate, and Stephen Levine is a trustworthy guide to the Universal Portal. Profoundly nourishing. A real treasure. Please discover and enjoy for yourself the pilgrimage of but a foot and a half—from head to heart. Absolutely #1."

—Gary Gach, author of *The Complete Idiot's Guide to Buddhism*
and founder of Mindfulness Fellowship

"Using the myths and image of Kuan Yin and her dragon mount, Stephen Levine has given us grace-filled meditations and reflections on the practice of a fierce compassion that constantly stretches the boundaries and limitations of what we previously thought was possible."

—Ralph Metzner, author of *The Unfolding Self*

"This book has a heart of its own. A boundless heart. A clarified heart. A heart that bridges humanity. A poetic reminder that enlightenment is not a head trip—it's a heart trip. I felt my own emotional armor shedding a little more with every page. A beauty-full read!"

—Jeff Brown, author of *Soulshaping*

"Kuan Yin smiles exquisitely in Stephen's writing. Blessings hide and seek between words and lines, eager to find and be found, console, heal, and inspire."

—Paul Cash

"I don't consider this wise and loving book as so much written by Stephen Levine as I do a clear message from Kuan Yin herself."

—John Fox, The Institute for Poetic Medicine and author of
Poetic Medicine: The Healing Art of Poem-Making

BECOMING
KUAN YIN

The Evolution *of* Compassion

Stephen Levine

WEISERBOOKS
San Francisco, CA / Newburyport, MA

First published in 2013 by Weiser Books, an imprint of
Red Wheel/Weiser, LLC
With offices at:
665 Third Street, Suite 400
San Francisco, CA 94107
www.redwheelweiser.com

Library of Congress Cataloging-in-Publication Data

Levine, Stephen, 1937–
    Becoming Kuan Yin : the evolution of compassion / Stephen Levine.
       pages cm
    ISBN 978-1-57863-555-9
    1. Avalokitesvara (Buddhist deity) I. Title.
    BQ4710.A8L48 2013
    294.3'4211—dc23   2013016705

Cover design by Nita Ybarra
Cover photograph © Maen CG / shutterstock
Author photo © Ondrea Levine
Interior by Dutton & Sherman Design
Typeset in Bembo text and Priori Sans and Centaur display
All photographs and line drawings © Ondrea Levine unless otherwise noted.

Printed in the United States of America
VG

10 9 8 7 6 5 4 3 2 1

The paper used in this publication meets the minimum requirements of the American
National Standard for Information Sciences—Permanence of Paper for Printed Library
Materials Z39.48-1992 (R1997).

CONTENTS

FOREWORD

When I first met Kuan Yin in a back street curio shop the owner described her as "she who hears the cries of the world." I was immediately drawn to her. Kuan Yin was the merciful guardian, the healer and protector of the suffering and disenfranchised. At that time I was working with the terminally ill, and I closely identified with her. She opened my heart. Taking her home with me that afternoon, I trusted so much what I felt that I never considered I'd need a book about her. Some people told me who she was thought to be, and that was enough.

Sometime later, I read John Blofeld's *The Bodhisattva of Compassion: The Mystical Tradition of Kuan Yin* and realized that her presence in the world had a profound resonance. So when Stephen told me he was going to work on a book about Kuan Yin and the emissaries of her compassion a few years ago, I was delighted. It was the natural expression of his decades of spiritual practice. It was going to be a doozy!

Once Stephen started writing, the words came as though delivered from the heavens. He was excited as he learned from the remarkable transmission, and it symbiotically affected our practice. Kuan Yin was the Mother of Mercy we had known for so long at the bedside of the dying, offering us an initiation into the universe of her heart.

Late every afternoon Stephen would read the day's work to me, and we both received it as our next teaching. We began to recite the *Kuan shih yin pusa* mantra, the locomotive for Kuan Yin's train, on which we were grateful passengers.

As Stephen continued his work of attempting to receive Kuan Yin's pure essence, imagining what it must have taken to bring the whole world into her heart, it opened our path of service even wider. Kuan Yin taught us to rehabilitate the word "mercy," to bring it back from the shadows of "have mercy on me a miserable sinner" and offer it as a cipher for the longing hearts we knew so well.

He included none of the miracle stories gathered around her image. Her struggle to become what she became was miracle enough. Her presence was sorely needed in this sick and injured, this weeping, world. We are honored to be counted among her students.

—ONDREA LEVINE

PREFACE

For years Kuan Yin's presence permeated our home. Images of her sent from friends, or as a muse from our son Noah, found niches in our home over the years. She personified our devotion to service and the mercy called for to be a whole human being. Ondrea and I had each met Kuan Yin before we met each other thirty-five years ago.

This book, composed of legend and practice, came like dictation mostly at four in the morning. Waking, I would act as an innocent bystander to what might be called grace. Line after line was read off as noted, the main phrases I hoped I would be able to remember when I arose. Sometimes, not wanting to interrupt my half-meditative/half-sleep state, I'd slip from my bed and sit on the floor with a flashlight and a notebook to transcribe what I could. If the material was opening too many doors at once for me to manage, I would leave for my computer in the next room and do my best to record the messages tumbling in the slipstream of thought.

It was a gift beyond measure.

ABOUT A DINGBAT

仁 is the Chinese character for "benevolence." It is the character that represents "person" combined with the number "2." Recognizing that when 2 are present, benevolence is a natural occurrence. Benevolence eases duality. It is one of the Maha Viharas, great abodes, of the true heart.

The images of Kuan Yin and friends that
appear in this story live in our home.

ACKNOWLEDGMENTS

To Ondrea, whose example inspired this writing.

And a wish to acknowledge with gratitude and loving-kindness those who led me this far: Rabbi Wolk, Gautama, Shivananda, Rudi, Vivekananda, Rama Krishna, Ram Dass, Sujata, Sharon Salzberg, Jack Kornfield, Joseph Goldstien, the Karmapa, His Holiness the Dalai Lama, Li Po, Tu Fu, Pu Tai, and Dooley.

And those friends who made this book come true, in particular Jan Johnson, who wrote me out the blue and said, "Send me what you have," and Gary Leon's editorial inner eye. And my comrades in her arms, Lee Quarnstrom, Gary Gach, Raghu, and Paul Cash.

Chapter I

KUAN YIN AND THE BEGINNING OF THE WORLD

Namo Kuan Shih Yin Pusa. "Hail to Kuan Yin bodhisattva."
To know Kuan Yin we need to let go of all that is unloved, judged, forged from old mind clingings. She is the unconditional love beyond the conditioned mind.

Some ancient force is called forth in surrendering hindrance after hindrance of our secret wretchedness and obvious suffering, to yield to the light of our Original Heart.

Behind most Asian temple great Buddhas, there is a curtain where a small Kuan Yin figure and an incense burner rest, and a comfortable place to sit in the dharma-field connects the supplicants' heart to the edgeless presence of her loving-kindness. And behind it all, the Buddha-nature—the foundation of our potential for liberation and the liberating of all sentient beings from suffering.

Opening the gate of Kuan Yin, we discover parts of ourselves almost too beautiful for words. The yearning for the direct experience of our luminescent nature.

Most who recognize her name consider Kuan Yin a celestial bodhisattva in the later Buddhist pantheon, and perhaps even its muse. Some consider her an immortal in the Taoist tradition. She responds to many sacred names: Avalokiteshvara, Tara, Chenrize, Mother Mary, the angelic Bernice, Isis perhaps, Krishna of course, and generically (and even genetically) as the Beloved. The essence that reveals our undifferentiated Oneness, which is the unconditioned mind, is not other than unconditional love.

Chapter 2

BUDDHA COMES
TO CHINA

For many hundreds of years the quality of devotion in Buddhism was mostly reserved for a profound thankfulness for Buddhadharma and meditational practice. Indeed, devotion was otherwise reserved for a beloved teacher, but little else.

When Siddhartha Gautama emerged as Buddha from beneath the bodhi tree, he said he taught only "the cause and end of suffering," mostly through a precise mindfulness. To this day, this is the basis of every Buddhist tradition following.

Decades after his original enlightenment and first teachings, Buddha's subsequent teachings, known as the Second Turning of the Wheel, expanded the already healthy heart of Buddhism. The extended teachings added various celestial representations of powerful states of mind, increasing people's familiarity with those same qualities mindfulness explored. These personifications of states of mind, afflictive and regenerative, were a skillful

means to stay in the middle of the often strenuous path of self- and communal liberation. For instance, the image of Manjushri on the ready, sword raised to subdue ogres and wrathful deities, represents cutting through or liberating the hindrances to the heart. And Tara, Avalokiteshvara, and, of course, Kuan Yin remind us of loving-kindness and compassion, forgiveness and equanimity.

This Mahayana school of Buddhism naturally employed the *Maha Viharas,* the great abodes of wisdom and service, such as mercy, gratitude, generosity, perseverance, devotion to practice, and sympathetic joy, which strengthen the liberation of the mind and the revelation of the heart.

Spreading from northern India down the Silk Road to parts east and China, these *Mahayana,* or "big raft" teachings, expanded by the further insights and interpretations of bodhisattva adepts, became the activation of the compasionate teaching to serve, to relieve the suffering of all sentient beings. The Mahayana school created some of Buddhism's most remarkable teachings, such as the Diamond Sutra, which came to be the foundation for a practice that acknowledged broader fields of awareness/reality, and deeper realms of reponsibility on which Buddhadharma was practiced. These included an intuitive mysticism, rights of empowerment, shamanic elements of healing practices, and the influence of mystery teachings, led by enlightened male and female masters that included but went beyond the earliest teachings.

In China, Kuan Yin gave form to the formless through the open lotus of her heart, enabling her to become "she who hears the cries of the world." She personifies the alleviation of suffering and became a major organizing factor in the widespread devotional element of Buddha's later teachings. The vow she took was, "For as long as space endures, and for as long as living beings remain, until then may I too abide to dispel the misery of the world."

Carried down the Silk Road into China, Kuan Yin became a profound spiritual and social influence that envisioned an ideal Pure Land, a perfect environment for the perfections of the practice's deepest work with increased concentration, illuminated by the heart, including an astral physical realm by some reckoning, a psychological reality certainly, and doubtlessly a matter of the heart, brought to the birth and deathbed.

In the Lotus Sutra there is the first recognition that women are capable of enlightenment. In the earliest, Indian years of Buddhism, the bodhisattva of compassion was housed in a male body, represented as Avalokita (short for Avalokiteshvara). Thus, Kuan Yin embodies both the male and female aspects that unite the whole.

Some say that Kuan Yin, having been male for centuries before being born in the Chinese collective consciousness in her present female form, created the perfect balance between yin and yang, anima and animus, which perfectly prepared her to be, as many believe, the Buddha of the present era. Kuan Yin is the first acknowledged female Buddha.

It is said that a bodhisattva can manifest in whatever form those in need can most easily perceive, in whatever form the teachings in compassion might require, whether male or female, young or old, of this world or another, ghost, dragon, fish, animal, bird, or even burning bush. She came to me as Kuan Yin. Elevated to the status of goddess by many grateful millions, she is revered for the light she has brought and the sense of protection she has instilled in many. She is seen as a safe harbor for the heart. The Lotus Sutra says that anyone, even a "lowly" caste person, can become liberated before some old Brahman busy playing with his gold toe ring if her whole heart is turned toward the well-being of others and compassion is acted upon.

The sutra also acknowledges that liberation is invited in by a gracious mercy. That the inborn spirit can be realized in a sudden overwhelming flash of clarity. It was a brand-new world of spiritual equality!

The Mahayana practices found a home in a variety of cultures, such as Vajrayana in Tibet and Zen in Japan. Kuan Yin and Buddhism, which was called the "Light of Asia," then crossed the great waters and was welcomed in all the Americas and Europe, as the Tibetan prophecy predicted: "When chariots run on rails and iron birds fly in the sky, the light will cross the sun heading west."

Chapter 3

THE ORIGIN
OF KUAN YIN

There are many accounts of Kuan Yin's origin, but the story that has the most versions is of Miao Shan, the compassionate daughter of a feared despot and usurper of the throne in another period of upheaval in China. Contemplating the writings of Lao Tzu, Confucius, Li Po, Chuang Tzu, and many other hearts and minds, Miao Shan came to sense their experience. A poet in her own right, she was absorbed in the writings of Gautama Buddha. The later Heart Sutra, attributed to Miao Shan's evolution into Kuan Yin, contains the *Prajna Paramita,* also known as the Kuan Yin Sutra, which is still chanted throughout the Buddhist world today.

Miao Shan was born into the Miao culture, known for its animistic reverence for all living things, which was the inherited basis of her spiritual memory.

As was the tradition of the Miao clan, a tree was planted at Miao Shan's birth and was to be cut down after she died to make her coffin. As she grew, the tree-like Miao Shan's *Ficus religiosa,* the bo tree, grew with her.

Though living in an atmosphere of anger and violence, Miao Shan nonetheless found time to slip away from the palace to walk in the forest, and in a sunlit clearing she would tend to a sapling she thought of as the Tree of Life, and all the sacred elements of nature that surrounded and nurtured it. Singing to it as the center of the forest spirits' mandala. Collecting stones from a nearby creek, she laid labyrinthine paths that spiraled out from the "heart" of the tree. She walked the paths each day, her songs and the pathways expanding outward from the center.

When her father presumed Miao Shan was having emotional crying fits during these frequent disappearances into the forest, she was actually in bliss and experiencing a profound interconnection with all of life.

As a child she was known to sit under the tree conversing with tigers and tiger lilies alike. Dogwood blossoms deepened her silk rug in mottled shadow. She loved most to lie secreted in dappled shadow as the light danced bright and soft through her dreams of a hallowed land for the animals she loved and protected. Her first dream of the worlds of consciousness awaiting.

Drawn at age 9.

Becoming Kuan Yin

Miao Shan thought she heard the big koi surfacing in the pond nearby with a word rising from its lips: "Remember." She always admired carp for their intelligence and straightforwardness. Fish seemed happier than most people.

Dragonflies dipped their long quills in the water and wrote poetic formulas for the benefit of the air aching for their music; the whir and hum of fairy-winged flashes of color braided the visiting lion's mane on the water's shimmering surface. Everything had a voice. The insects, fish, and pond had their own music. Miao Shan sang harmony.

Injured birds fluttered broken-winged onto her blanket, waiting. Their small, hollow bones of flight joined and set almost instantaneously, as if time was malleable in her cupped hands open in prayer for their next flight in or out of their body.

Though just a child, somehow she understood. She recognized how fragile life was, and how much compassion hurt. Her hands soft as down soothed the birds as they healed or died, both in the light of her patient kindness.

Wild things came close then halted, not out of fear, but in reverence to her reverie, not wanting to interrupt. When she raised her head, fox and jackrabbit, bobcat and bullfrog approached as original supplicants before the sun. Breathing quietly, Miao Shan listened to each unique lyric with a heart that could hear the sorrow of the world. Sometimes they inadvertently harmonized, making her giggle, the dark green spears of the leaves above fluttering in her world-blessing out breath.

The few people who were allowed by edict near her marveled at how lighthearted a child she was, considering the dark pall that permeated the palace.

Drawn at age 14.

Oblivious to her despotic father, Miao Shan handfed the deer in the courtyard, usually followed about by a sizable wild boar whose broken leg she had wrapped in bamboo leaves and set with a silk ribbon. His slight limp endeared him to her all the more. It was quite a sight to see Miao Shan and her animal friends resting together by the stream, to see the wild boar snoring loudly on one side of her, his foot in her lap, while the tiger she had raised from a cub, considerably bigger than herself by then, stretched out and purred against her on the other.

In the fall of her ninth year, dozing in the moonlight, a small emerald-green grass snake seeking warmth curled up under her arm and remained motionless until she was awoken by one of the palace staff. Miao Shan thought it quite lovely, and, holding it lightly in her palm, she smuggled it up into her bedroom. Putting Greenie in the shirt pocket of her silk pajamas, she laid on her back to sleep, telling her thoughts to wake her if she started to roll over, which might injure this beautiful creature. Several times she woke during the night as her shoulder started to turn against the mattress but her heart awoke her. In the morning her smooth green friend remained resting quietly in the bottom of her shirt pocket.

They maintained what seemed to her an ongoing friendship for weeks, as he taught her to remain perfectly still even in her sleep. It was her first yoga. She fed him ant eggs until she could free him to glide through the fragrant grass. An initiation from so small a creature in so big a world, Greenie slid away beneath the tree, always to remain in Miao Shan's heart. Having learned something about controlling the mind and how precious stillness could be.

There are many stories of Miao Shan's relationships with reptiles and other creatures whose hearts stayed closest to the ground, an energy transference from ancient India's mystical *nagas*—the energy channels through the human body and the living earth—often represented as the great cobras protectively hooding deities such as Shiva. And of course the most spiritually energetic of them all, with whom Miao Shan had a lifelong relationship, were the benevolent South Sea dragons.

After her transmigration into the celestial bodhisattva Kuan Yin, it was rumored that she often came to people as animals in their dreams to encourage them to be emissaries of her compassionate protection of the earth. She occasionally appeared as a golden snake—frightening at first but then endearing—to demonstrate the fear of nature and eventually the love of its boundless beauty. The theme of fear mutating into love was a very common teaching she provided to many. She also came at times as a tiger or panther to demonstrate the possibility of loving-kindness gentling the wilderness between the heart and the mind, surrendering all that limits further entrance into what lies beyond.

As Miao Shan approached her teens, she could be heard in her room reciting a beloved *gatha,* slightly chanting or singing a hymn. Her father, despising his daughter's absorption in spiritual matters, indeed a sovereign with considerable blood on his hands, feared, seeing her tending the forest animals, said derisively she might "go native" if she didn't soon marry "a strong military man." He wanted sons, his other two daughters having disappointingly given birth to "only" females, and he wanted an heir to the throne soon!

Her father, trying to break Miao Shan to his will, forced her to do what he considered "slave work," to clean out the slop of the stables, which the richer members of his court had considered foul abuse but for her was a blessing. Miao Shan loved horses. And to further get her to do his bidding, to marry as he insisted even though it was against her better sense, he pushed her into the kitchen to work with the actual slaves (prisoners of war and discarded concubines). But her removal from the luxuries of the palace, rather than filling her with the intended self-pity, instead cultivated in her a profound empathy for her abused co-workers, another level of kinship with those in distress whom she did all she could to support.

Her concern for the kitchen and stable workers, helping as she might with their work, and listening to the sorrows of those "beneath" her, only reinforced the king's rage that she was in severe need of "a strong man who would make her obedient to her high office." He felt too that Miao Shan might as well be dead if she would not accede to his demands, his last chance of procuring a male heir to maintain his lineage. But this was not to be, as she went against the common social fascism that daughters were to be married off to suit the father's alliances and sons were to die in battle. And he pondered what more might be done to bend her to his determination.

Miao Shan awoke one morning after a dream of celestials beckoning her to come close, embracing her. She experienced what she had always known, that this infinite love of inborn divinity was the enormity given her to distribute to a suffering world. Overcome by ecstasy, she could have floated free to heaven realms, but felt she could not leave the earth alone any more than one would abandon a helpless child.

She knew the monastic life was her only option. Though others, dazed with desire, wished for romance, it seemed to her that she naturally longed for the deep silence that convened with the spirit. While her sisters fantasized about young captains and tall princes, she wondered about the nature of the bodhisattva's heart. She did not need to choose further.

Miao Shan didn't think in terms of happiness but of the fulfillment she experienced while helping others, and retreated into the bowels of the palace, where she met slaves and workwomen alike who toiled under the threat of violence if they did not perform to the pleasure of the guards and especially her father. Though reticent at first, her honesty and kindness allowed her to work with the ailing workwomen in the dark kitchen at the stoves and cooking pits. Bringing to the weak and ill each day whatever medicines and ointments, food and tonics she could gather. Then having to sneak back up to her room late at night to wash the soot off her face and bathe before dawn. She also found it strengthened her heart to work in the stables when she got the chance, close to the animals and workers she so admired. Each day her resolve grew stronger to become a renunciant and live the life of one who commits to the perfection of the spirit.

Becoming Kuan Yin

Chapter 4

MIAO SHAN
AT THE GATE

Strongly opposed to his daughter's commitment to taking up the spiritual life, the king forbade Miao Shan from leaving the palace. She appealed to him to let her follow her natural way, but he proclaimed his absolute rule to follow his twisted version of filial piety or be a thankless, cursed child.

When she still denied her father's demand to marry and bear sons to uphold the power of his dynasty, the king composed a revenge. He sought some hellish domain in which to break her spirit. But she insisted she would not take a husband and wished only to follow her own path.

Bombarded by his insistence that she marry, she appeared at last to relent and said she would indeed marry under the condition that he find her a husband who could tell her how she might overcome the suffering of illness, old age, and inevitable death.

When the king of course could not find any man to fulfill her requirements, crimson-faced at not being able to dissuade her from her piety, he forced the abbess of a local convent, under threat that he would burn the nunnery to the ground if she did not comply, to accept Miao Shan as a neophyte and torture her until she broke. To give her the foulest, most vile tasks they could devise, wishing her a life so repugnant she would rush home to do his bidding. And the frightened nuns, on threat of their convent being destroyed, did their best to make Miao Shan's life a living hell, and being a nunnery of five hundred, they had many an opportunity.

Miao Shan unknowingly, gladly accepted this opportunity to enter a spiritual retreat. She was given a tiny, barren, windowless cell with a cold stone floor for a bed. Instructed to wash the last speck of gray dust from the old stone walls of all the buildings, almost blinded by the sharp stone specks that rained down with each swipe of the brush, she persevered for many weeks and was then additionally ordered to do garbage duty each morning and every evening before she could retreat into sleep. She cleaned the latrines and animal pens, and finally she was instructed, fatigued or not, to tend to the many sick and dying old nuns.

Most nights she was woken abruptly from her exhausted sleep to care for sick monastics, to continually empty their bedpans and wipe the blood, pus, and vomit from the floor. At first she was dismayed and had to numb herself to the penetrating stench of their illnesses. She would even wretch at times when the swill in the bedpans spilled over her hands. She saw what a "privileged" life she had been accustomed to and realized, like Siddhartha renouncing his palace and finding himself in a wretched, suffering world, that only by delving deeper into her innate spiritual memory could she be free of aversion and unhappiness. And she began to experience the flickering joy of the renunciation recommended by the sutras.

Gradually, entering these sick rooms reeking of poorly attended illness no longer repulsed her but began smelling of helplessness and need. As her initial resistance fell away and she became more present in the room, she saw the shadowy figures in the beds had eyes, faces, trembling hands from which she had previously retreated that reached out, requiring little more than human touch. Her heart split open.

Dumping the bedpans, she soon noticed their dreadful contents actually smelled different from one to the next; their contents even looked slightly different. And she began to look into their substance by window light, and recognizing one odor from another, some slightly metallic, others dark with blood, and each took on a category of need.

She asked the old nuns she attended to what they knew of traditional Chinese medicine to understand what herbs, roots, barks, fungus, and leaves might reach the cause of bloody bowels, excessive diarrhea, feces that had turned white, and urine turned black. And when the chance arose, she would slide into the forest to pick what herbs she felt might be of some help. She would grind the herbs in the secret of night, making a concoction to relieve pain, slow the encrustation of open sores, loosen dried crust around the nostrils, or provide a blessed sleep to those she had some sense she might be of some aid. She would patiently administer potions to the gray figures whose faith in the sisterhood was holding them in slight stead, as infection and the dissolution of organs left them alone with only their feeling of failure and disappointment that those they had prayed to for so long had abandoned them.

Miao Shan also read what she could find about energy points on the body she might administer pressure to to soothe the pain or reduce the nausea, but she felt her helplessness, and her love and prayers, were all she could give in the midst of her inability to relieve their prodigious difficulty.

Drawing pus from dying nuns' rampant bedsores, she began to sing to them of the dharma-field, the *Brahmaloka* (abode of the dharma kings), Pure Land where the ideal conditions for practice and fruition were effortlessly available. And sometimes their pain dropped away and she wondered if they had gotten a glimpse or even intuited something wondrous beyond their long sickness and the ravages of old age.

The song occasionally became a chant, a slow emanation from the heart of her wish for their well-being. In one room chanting for hours to a slowly dying woman, she thought dawn had come much earlier than expected, filling the room with a glow by which she could make out even the most delicate features of the nascent

Amitabha on the scroll above her bed. But when she looked up from her patient's softening face, night was still pressed against the windowpane. And Miao's hands, so smeared with the detritus of holding the dying woman's hands, felt suddenly clean, as though she held celestial hands. She wondered if, for just a moment, the poor woman experienced something like that too, which might have given confidence that even in death she would not be alone.

And she wept not from the pain in the room but for the bliss that penetrated their hearts. And when she looked into the woman's eyes, which had for hours been strained with pain and the hope for a quick end, there was an unmistakable peace. And there the two of them, in the midst of hell, were immersed in grace.

When the old nun died, Miao Shan gently washed her body while singing to her of her true nature, building with each soft breath a raft to carry her to the other shore, on which Miao Shan could imagine a sacred abode where the nun could finish all she had begun.

Chapter 5

MIAO SHAN OBSERVING

Miao Shan was learning a lot about true prayer and the levels of loving-kindness meditation available in surrender and mindful service as they infiltrated each action throughout her day. She found her heart in the first breath upon waking, and it called forth her spiritual ancestors, the saints, bodhisattvas, and Buddhas of the ages for support.

Each intention was enforced with the clarity and power of love. She learned more about love by watching how unloving the people around her could be. She learned about how mercy could heal, like a poultice, the wounds of absence in the convent's sad inhabitants. And the parishioners, many out of exasperation, came to plead their causes to some power beyond their own. Some bemoaned their losses, bent ruined by life in a hard world, and sat in the midst of their grief as they beseeched their personal gods to intercede in their ongoing difficulty without consideration of their own divinity. Miao Shan prayed they would understand the cleansing power of forgiveness as she gave them a prayer to repeat: "The power of God, of love, is within me; the power of God, of love, surrounds me." Other parishioners, having begun that opening practice some while before, sat nearby in near ecstasy, just glad to be alive. It gave her, she thought later, some insight about freeing people from hell as well as freeing those in heaven from not taking it for granted.

She noticed too that as people gained more capacity to hold their pain in their hearts, their prayers became less out of need than out of gratitude, and the desire to serve others less a request than an offering.

Watching the long, labored breath of the dying, she learned how to breathe. How much there was in each breath—so much, so much—worlds of mind and matter in each inhalation, each exhalation. That the breath was not just one, two, and three. That there were innumerable fractions between one and two. And that before each in breath and out breath, there arose a motivating intention to take that breath, and release that breath. That before each and every action there was a decision to move forward.

In meditation, watching closely, she concentrated on how the world changes within the breath, noting precisely how thoughts and feelings attempted to seduce her away from her goal. She investigated that which interfered so the mind did not obstruct the heart.

And she found that noting the intentions at the beginning and end of each breath kept her even more focused on her purpose. And, most wonderfully, this recognition of intention, a choice, before action purified her actions

Becoming Kuan Yin

and seemed to clear much of what many refer to as karma (which she defined as simply "momentum").

Able to enter her original heart, she was getting the teaching from every nook and cranny.

She heard chanting everywhere—in the main hall and the shadowed recesses of the monastery, at the edge of the forest and the nearby mountain huts. The jewel in the lotus grew everywhere and took root in her bones, in her flesh, in the space between her breaths, as the Prajna Paramita Heart Sutra blossomed in her original dream. She listened to the mantras coming down the dusty road as paeans drifted in from camelback and holy pilgrims came to water and rest. Recitations of distant holy books in languages she did not understand magically helped them cross the bridge to other worlds.

She learned from the old mendicant monks who emerged from the forest to practice their contemplations before an image of the Compassionate One, quieted by their grace. They sat at the edge of creation, mirroring the equanimity out of which the world and mind are created from moment to moment.

Some monks not entering the monastery sat in the courtyard in meditative prayer seeking not some Supreme Being but supreme *beingness;* doing spiritual practice not just for their own benefit, but for the well-being of others, for peace and healing, or for forgiveness, sending loving-kindness to all sentient beings.

A few months into attending to the old nun Dipananda, who seemed to have an advanced brain tumor, Miao Shan saw the old woman was beginning to experience considerable head pain. She had been getting a little aphasic, scrambling her words due to wobbly brain connections. "My words are all broken and tossed without holy order in the air," she said.

"How remarkable," Dipananda said during one of her clearer moments. "Me, leading prayers, singing liturgies, guiding the group for forty years. They used to call me the 'song mother,' and now my offering to the celestials is like a broken mala, the prayer beads scattered hither and yon. My prayers have fallen apart. They make no sense at all. Please pray with me."

Miao said to her beloved friend, "Maitreya Buddha Mother holds you in her arms. She knows your heart. The love you share goes well beyond words. No offering greater than love."

As the pressure in Dipananda's head increased, she writhed back and forth on her bed, her mouth dry, beads of perspiration on her forehead, shaking with pain. Sitting next to her, Miao Shan followed her hard-pained breath into the vast unknown. Breathing in, she melted into the boundless compassion of Dipankara, (a Buddha who reached enlightenment twenty-four eons before, according to Gautama, the current historical Buddha), after whom the old nun was named. Breathing out, she embraced the dying nun in the arms of the universal quality of "that which is called to the cries of the world," whose presence was palpable in the evening shadow. Miao Shan prayed that the great vastness might float Dipananda free of the vise-like pressure.

She sat quietly and began to sing into the nun's heart. Not knowing what else to do but extend from her death-less center the peace gathering in the room. Kneeling beside the old woman, from beyond herself she whispered in her ear, "Dipa, the Beloved, the angel of mercy is beside you."

Suddenly the gravity in the room changed. The old woman's face softened as the pain-induced heaviness departed. She went into what appeared to be pure ecstasy.

And for a few hours the energy, the "glow," was so intense that each nun coming to wish her safe passage could not enter without feeling engulfed by an overwhelming, effusive joy. The room suffused with a golden light, the original light at the center of all things. All were bathed in the luminosity that illuminates the original heart. All day long, others came and sat and chanted softly around the nun's bed. Her room becoming an ordained chapel.

When later offered pain medication by a physician she refused it, motioning the gathering assemblage away with a soft, silent hand. Apparently not wanting to disturb or degrade her experience of the presence.

Miao Shan wept not for the pain in the room but for the bliss that penetrated all their hearts. And when she looked into the woman's eyes, which earlier had been dulled with pain, there was now an unmistakable peace. The two immersed in grace, embraced by the One; the two of them in the midst of seeming hell, immersed in paradise.

When the rest of the nuns and the reluctant abbess entered the room, expecting the sour air of descending mortality, they instead encountered a circle of dozens of luminous young and older women whose faces were radiant with the energy emanating from the collective heart, the shared heart of the Divine, resonating with the yearning for the radiance of our true nature, unconditional love. This seeing through of death serves the devotional aspect of the hidden mysteries, well beyond definition but not beyond experiencing the Oneness we call the Beloved.

Sitting by Dipa's side, coordinating the tides of her breath with the old woman's as one might aid a person giving birth—"chanting at the gate," as Miao Shan put it—she sang the old woman out of her body as she gradually ceased breathing and slipped away. In the third watch of the night Miao gently washed the old body, singing to her of her true nature.

Like the slow recession of a great tide, the convent settled into a deep silence as the shared breath of the young and old released the tension in their bodies so as to do nothing to hold Dipa back. And continuing to chant, Miao Shan slowly wrapped the empty body in clean linen.

The young Kuan Yin-to-be, closer than ever to the heart of the matter, all matter.

　　　　　　　　　　　　　　Becoming Kuan Yin

It became a ritual for Miao Shan to, when awoken from heavenly visions, attend to the weak and dying, to sing whatever sutra her heart suggested—perhaps their favorite, she sometimes mused as she cleaned their worn bodies. The touch of a merciful hand a blessing to their physical and psychological wounds. Wiping their tear-stained cheeks, she reminded the ailing nuns to trust their light and share their healing with all the others going through this same ordeal.

Taking each breath with them, breathing their breath into her body, she received something from each abandoned sister and forgotten mother, each supplicant who had lost her prayer to a withering brain. Letting them know, after a life of failure and success dedicated most often to mercy and awareness, that they did not need to be different in any way to be received by their spiritual ancestors. To release themselves from the need for perfection and to trust the merciful process.

Many of the dying called for her. She was becoming that angel.

The songs Miao Shan sang of the benevolent Pure Land dragons playing with the pearl of great wisdom reminded some nuns of the lullabies their mothers sang to them as children. And sometimes the angels of mercy in the song began to chant along with her as hours passed in the profound softness of a dying loved one's hand; the chant slowing and becoming a whisper as the holy old body was put aside.

And she spoke to them of other worlds, the realms of liberation, of completed practice, that waited in the core of Being. Of their perfect inherent nature manifest on the mountains and rivers walked in mindful meditation, of halls filled with departed spirits comforted in a noble silence produced from a collective concentration many times greater than the norm, piercing the veil to "see as God sees."

And as they passed, the song became a chant—*Gate gate paragate parasamgate bodhi swaha.* "Gone, gone beyond, gone altogether beyond, liberation hail!"—which she would eventually include, as Kuan Yin, in her transmission of the Prajna Paramita Heart Sutra, the startling clarity of the perfection of wisdom. The chant going lower by the hour, Miao Shan's breath coordinated with theirs, undifferentiated; one breath, one mind, one heart.

And when she was called to wrap putrid corpses, she held them and rocked them as if each were her only child. Singing hymns and lullabies, and chanting the great mantra of liberation as it rose up her spine.

When she heard that her charge was reveling in what was supposed to be a hellish domain, the abbess feared for her own life. The king would surely cut off her head unless Miao Shan's life was sufficiently unbearable. She devised that Miao should be there for the most wretched of all: to attend to the inconsolable lamentations of young women who had been beaten or raped and run to the monastery for sanctuary. And so Miao Shan additionally turned to listen to the worst hours of these women's lives and breathed again and again through the aching grief point in the center of her chest, clearing the conduit to her heart so as to embrace those in such unspeakable pain in the mysteriously calming compassion of her Buddha-nature, the mercy of the ever-born Avalokiteshvara. Blanketing them with the cloak of compassion that love can offer. And when some grief-stricken child who had been sexually assaulted laid her head on Miao Shan's shoulder, she became the Mother of Mercy.

After frightfully maintaining the house rules of cruelty to the sovereign's daughter for years, the nuns thought Miao Shan would break at any moment. Not knowing they had answered her inquiry about how to live with sickness, old age, and death with an open heart. Fulfilling her wish for completion, she rose gladly from the cold floor eager to serve the suffering and hold the hands of those in misery engulfed in a merciless world. Her compassion expanded with each embrace of suffering until at last they did not need to rouse her, as they found her already meditating or waiting at the bedside or the monastery door to welcome the grieving. Sometimes even listening at the nuns' own doors when they wept for their doubt and lack of faith.

And filled with dedication to the healing of all sentient beings in this world needing the poultice of loving-kindness, she took the bodhisattva vow: "For as long as

Chapter 6

MIAO SHAN
IN HELL

The king, expecting Miao Shan to come scratching at his door begging for his forgiveness and ready to marry whomever he chose, was frustrated that his plan seemed not to be working. When more than a year had passed he became furious and demanded of the abbess an excuse for not executing his orders. The abbess replied that she had often asked Miao if she was ready to go back to the ease of her palace, but said she was repeatedly rebuffed by the young woman who said she had at last found her home. Hearing that she wanted to live as she was without changing any of the conditions required of her, only to remain in the convent for as long as possible, he became enraged. Driven to distraction, he cut down Miao Shan's bo tree and ordered her execution.

However, something in Miao Shan's resolution to her cause radiated from her body, causing the executioner to fail—blunted the axe, broke the sword, snapped the spear, and finally turned the garrote to a garland. Her father

ordered the executioner be executed for not carrying out his commands. (Here some tales speak of a celestial tiger interceding to take her body away from harm, but it seems more likely that it was the power of profound compassion that protected her.)

But knowing it was no fault of her vassal, Miao Shan dropped her body and assumed the guise of death, as we all must, to protect the distraught executioner from punishment. Taking on the karmic debt of her executioner and even, it is generously added, her father alike, to save them from due torment. Her father's obscene violence absorbed in her boundless compassion, the executioner's tears cupped in her thin hands, she allowed the gravity of their actions to draw her into hell.

Becoming Kuan Yin

There is no greater love than the love it takes to save others from themselves, either here or hereafter. Indeed, is Jesus not most revered because it is said he died for others' sins? Even an atheist, believing in none of the rumors or folklore or even superstition of religion, can respect that intention, that guileless state of mind that cares for others even more than for oneself. Is there any more sufficient definition of love than mercy?

And as she dropped into a barren hell, Miao Shan saw, as in the monastery, what pulled people into such dreadful environments. That perhaps no other world needed forgiveness more than this one. She wept when she saw what damage their mercilessness, avarice, grasping, and violence had done to themselves and others. How they were being crushed against their better knowing. All their wounded masks and broken nerve ends numbed, all the mercilessness with themselves and others that kept them unable to stand up straight, that kept them from becoming human once again, broke her heart into a thousand pieces, dispersing her light through the darkness. And her compassion, illuminating the delusions that made them believe they deserved to suffer, drawing them into her boundless heart.

And the tormented around her pleaded for forgiveness. And feeling that all deserved a salve for their shame and self-loathing, she taught them how to forgive and be forgiven; how to release the holding around the heart that could not let go of anger and vengeful feelings toward others and themselves. She encouraged them to speak into the hearts of those they may have injured through word, action, even thought, and ask for forbearance of their unwholesome acts; then she forgave them for those moments when they could not yet see.

In hell she taught mindfulness of the present, where all the feelings that assault the mind and tear at the heart reside, where all the emotional afflictions find their home. She said to instead find from moment to moment your heart's awareness of what's happening while it's happening—which, we heard one convict say, when encouraged to mindfully investigate his pain, fear, anxiety, and remorse, his suffering, was more painful to endure than his nine years spent on death row.

She taught the denizens to have compassion for themselves and others, to reach through themselves to the inmate next door. She said that in some ways hell was one of the most supportive places to practice, because the cause and possible end of suffering were so evident. A like-minded community of lost souls reconnecting with themselves, cultivating a loving-kindness that might be offered to others.

She offered the heart's balance to the wretchedness of the mind when she told them that the Buddha said, "You could look the whole world over and never find anyone more deserving of love than yourself." And they wept and could not stop the tears. The first step of cleansing underway.

She said to continue the remarkable practices for a few years, and the rest of your life. And remember to add to your forgiveness those who you injured, harmed, and left bereft of trust in the world. Say to them, "I ask your forgiveness for whatever I may have done to you, intentionally or unintentionally, that caused you to forget your innate beauty or diminished your wonder." And perhaps someday you may be able to turn to yourself, and calling yourself by your own first name, say, "I forgive you."

It takes eons to be whole. Miao Shan even forgave hell for existing.

She gave breath to the mindful transformation that encouraged forgiveness of themselves so they might go teach this great mercy to others. "Oh, what we do to each other!" some exclaimed as the cause of suffering, and the potential end of suffering sank in.

As they continued, their hearts slowly began to open, touching the stony ground, she called the earth to witness, opening the eye of beauty as forests burst from fertile soil, flowers splashing color across the canvas of their minds, bright rivers and stately mountains blessing lightning crossing the sky. Sunrise for those who came to long for the heart and could hear. And for those who once "could not yet see," they saw.

After some time her presence had entered so many that the wretched heard meandering through the once-fetid air—a song. Perhaps their original song. Music not heard for millennia quenched the flames of hell, the lotus blossom of the dharma rising from the embers. And the old demons, whose eyes had become so accustomed to the darkness were no longer so deaf and blind; they were relieved enough to recognize what needed to be done next to find heaven buried nearly out of sight in their hearts. It was as Meister Eckhart, the remarkable Christian monk of the Middle Ages, had commented: He would prefer a hell with Jesus to a heaven without.

And the song made its way through the forests and down the alleys, healing its way through the hopelessness, and offering a harmonic to the confident luminosity of the original heart. Sitting in purifying silence, they sought out their misanthropy and crimes against others, and poured mercy over the fires. And their fire became water, and the water was their holy water pulling them out and upward.

Pouring mercy into the darkness, Miao Shan becoming the bodhisattva Kuan Yin.

She liberated hell, singing:

Old stories, legends of creation,
won't keep Hades from becoming paradise.
Rumi said for the person who loves the truth
"Their water is fire."
He made spring out of winter.
He learned from his mistakes.
There were moments
when numb from thinking
we forget we pass through hell
on our way to heaven.

Becoming Kuan Yin

And if that heavenly glow
does not distract us
too much, dehypnotized by grace,
we continue past heaven
into the boundless enormity
which dwarfs it.

There was much consternation on the part of Yama, Lord of the Underworld, the presiding bureaucrat, upon recognizing the effect of the Mother of Mercy's presence in hell. Fearing if she remained he would lose his civil service job, he immediately transported her away, exiling her to the island of Putuoshan, in the Zhoushan Archipelago of the South China Sea.

Having turned great tragedy into considerable opportunity, the residents of the underworld were freed to approach heaven. Turning the flames to flowers, removing the greed and mercilessness from their eyes, Kuan Yin offered them protective mantras and sacred songs to pass on the healing to a better world. Turning hell to paradise, perhaps seeding the earth with the early incarnations of those who would themselves eventually take the bodhisattva vow. How many kind and gentle births may have been germinated in breaking free from hell?

There is, by the way, another anecdote about Kuan Yin's passing through hell. The judiciary panel in hell wanted to see for themselves if the rumors of her sanctity and magnanimity could be maintained when confronted with boundless suffering, so they drew her close enough to receive her blessing, that they too might return to earth without the forgetfulness that brought these judges down in the first place.

Because she protected her rights as a woman and defied marrying against her will just to give birth to an heir, Kuan Yin is considered the guardian of rights for women—and all people, actually—to choose their inborn path, as well as the guardian of childbirth.

As women's guardian, she whispered in the left ear of pregnant women that they were the center of the Wheel of Life, the quintessential alchemists who drew the elements together in their womb by which the seed is watered and breathes, that they were the Luminous. And she sang to embryos in the womb, told them wild healing stories, and imbued their genes with a tendency toward mercy.

Women had been wife-destined chattel, their mates chosen by their fathers often as business negotiations. A son's birthright the coffins of war or the chains of slavery being their predominant options until Kuan Yin offered an alternative to this totalitarian convention. By refusing marriage, much less childbearing, she was the exemplar of one following her perfect Tao, a spirit committed to clearing the hindrances to liberation.

Kuan Yin had entered hell a vow-taker and departed a bodhisattva, a spiritual hero whose primary practice is clear-minded, open-hearted service to all sentient beings, defining the total commitment of one's spiritual practice not only to one's own liberation but also to the freedom of all sentient beings, in every form, on every plane. Acting from a level of awareness that serves to liberate all beings while knowing there is nothing essentially separate from the enormity of Being.

Exiled from hell to the paradise of Fragrant Island, sacred Mount Putuo, breathing into the grief point of the world that had become the touch point of the heart, she sent compassion and loving-kindness out into all sentient beings.

> May all beings be free of fear
> and confusion, May we be liberated
> from hell, rising toward the light.
> May all the vow-takers and bodhisattvas
> waiting between heaven and hell
> find ample birth; and that the prayer,
> which cannot but amplify such duality,
> subside into the One.

Her shawl thrown over the supplicant, she bids grace rise to the surface.

Chapter 7

EXILED TO PARADISE

Climbing the sacred mountain, Kuan Yin surveyed the glistening world. Repeating the *gayatri,* acknowledging to the senses of all sentient beings in original mind from which all matter is devised, "Earth, Sky, Stars, Behold the Sun source of light from the heart of the Source, May it shape our minds."[1]

Then sitting motionless on a mountain ledge, guarded by two ancient junipers, she meditated for ten years. Cultivating mercy for all sentient beings as the earth built up around her and luxuriant grasses grew taller than her head. Embracing the world in boundless compassion.

Miao Shan sat in a sun-marked bit of ground on a cliff near the edge of the sea and took an oath not to move until she had become one with the constituents of mind and body, earth and sky.

---

1. A translation provided by Gary Snyder some years ago.

On Putuoshan the bodhisattva vowed not to move until the heart of heaven had become one with the human heart. Passing through the seasons, the wind-blown leaves, strips of bark, and drifting soil collecting about her caused her form to become less distinct. Passing through the years until only the boundlessness remained, her meditation blanket the earth accumulating around her, embracing her, a great grassy mound on which dragons often rested. She was a buried relic. Mountains and rivers were her nature. Absorbed in absolute silence, immersed in compassion for all sentient beings.

Having left Miao Shan to the guardians of the earth element she fulfilled her awakening and stood, covered in meadow, a Buddha of Infinite Compassion. Freed of time and form, she initiated the worthy as emissaries of world-healing compassion and snuck blessings into our dreams to offer merciful guidance to the heart of the mind.

Emerging from her cocoon, offering to all the opportunity called the bodhisattva vow, which might allow approach to the fulfillment of the momentum referred to as karma.

The bodhisattva Kuan Yin, sitting at rest in the dharma, emerged from her years of radiant stillness, Kuan Yin Buddha saying, "Before the Buddha are the bodhisattvas and vow-takers who commit themselves through this life and those that might come to act for the benefit of all sentient beings, taking the bodhisattva vow. I will give you now the vow as presently generated in me by all the compassionate Buddhas."

Have mercy on all sentient beings
keep their well-being at heart.
Take every opportunity to find
benefit for others.

Beings warm-blooded and cold
are numberless; I vow to aid them.
Illusions of separateness are innumerable;
I vow to awaken with them.

As long as there is suffering
I commit to protect with mercy and awareness
those who cannot yet see or be seen,
to enlighten myself for the benefit
    of all sentient beings.

To better hear the cries of the unheard
to better see the work to be done.
In the open heart and clear mind
for as long as suffering endures,
may I abide to dispel the delusion
and misery of the world.

During the millennia that followed, Kuan Yin meditated on the well-being of the world, having emptied the illusion that results in birth and death, like all the Buddhas that had preceded her.

In almost every spiritual prototype we have to go through hell on our way to pure awareness, indistinguishable from unconditional love, the Pure Land of our illuminated nature. For some, that process of awakening and "enlightening" is the experience the Taoists call "self ablaze."

Because she had attained unrestricted wisdom and compassion, it was difficult for many people to imagine Kuan Yin was just the human she actually was, shedding a million tears through as many lives, giving birth to every thought, and dying each and every death.

As the manifestation of nearly unimaginable compassion, reaching out to all beings in need, Kuan Yin is sometimes depicted as having a thousand arms. But perhaps her radiance sometimes blinds us to the actuality that it is not innumerable arms extending from the "nimbus of light" surrounding her, but her unremitting intention to receive each call and prayer and cry directed toward her. These seeming arms, these rays of light, also initiate the thousands of emissaries of compassion that the direct experience of loving-kindness motivates. The light that embraces returned a thousandfold. The succor of a bodhisattva mother.

And as legend goes she is also credited with having many heads, as in the form of some Indian gods. This I imagine is due to being able to hear on all levels, in every direction, the cries of the needy. Yet from many personal accounts of those apparently saved from the threat of death, many speak of her appearing full-faced before them. Even in the throngs of spiritual festivals, those who have encountered her speak of being looked into directly.

And naturally, sometimes she is attributed with having a thousand eyes. Of course she has a thousand eyes, as would any diligent mother.

Compassion reveals insight into the cause and end of suffering. Kuan Yin is recognized for this sense of liberation in the mind and lightness of the body. Inviting Kuan Yin into our pain invokes our original heart, the unfettered grace of our inherent nature.

To become Kuan Yin is to recognize the extreme toil and commitment that brings fruition. Her accomplishment not bestowed on her by some celestial prize committee, Zeus, or the Holy Ghost, but by the hard-earned forgoing of all earthly pleasure, to complete what Buddha called "the work to be done."

In a world, a mind, a body at war, no quality active or passive is more healing than essential compassion.

Without mercy there can be no peace.

Mercy is a forgotten necessity rarely considered. Corrupted by misuse. In need of rehabilitation, used to mercilessly intensify shame, and self-negation, like "Have mercy on me, a miserable sinner." It had been demagnetized.

When Kuan Yin heard mercy had been drained of its power to uproot suffering and bestow joy, she wept and revived its meaning in the teachings of her way.

Kuan shih yin pusa, the calling out, the repetition of her name, the mantric locomotive of Kuan Yin bodhisattva/Kuan Yin Buddha endeavors, from tens of millions each day, to reach her perfect hearing.

Becoming Kuan Yin

Chapter 8

THE ORIGIN
OF SONG

Having freed the demons to take the bodhisattva path and, filled with considerable joy, Kuan Yin opened all hearts to fill with mercy and compassion of their Origin of Song. The song embedded in the first gene of consciousness waiting to take birth.

Kuan Yin said "the song" that inspired evolution and took eons to develop the art of self-discovery. The song we need to sing for ourselves that at first is more felt than heard. In the beginning of each of our worlds, the song has no words, but words follow with recognition and praise, words of expectation and delight that resonate with trust in the process and a delight in not knowing what comes next.

Before the Buddha, before even "I am," a song was reflected in fire, in water, in air. A birth song arose uninvited from a handful of earth. Something more than rational could see a melody written in the solar system sequestered at the center of each tree.

In the flickering rhythms of fire were our first meditations. But even before fire was corralled to the fire pit, there were wild, insightful contemplations by a stream and a peace that surpassed understanding in the rustling of windblown trees. And the monotheism of the earth only the heart could discern rose up to meet our feet when we danced. When lightning blinded the night between stars, it knew there were forces we could hardly name. Echoing through infinity in our bones, it beckoned the spirit forward.

Gliding through the phylum of the womb, gills sealed, the chest anointed with breath, we have become aware we are aware. Engaged in evolution, containing the history of the procession humming in our cells.

All spirituality, and eventually religion, may well have originated in deserts, forests, and secluded caves, from the inordinate but natural occurrence of spontaneous body-shaking, mind-glistening, spirit-revealing, mystical uprisings. Profound releases from within giving rise to prophecy and healing powers. It was the discovery of our original fire.

When, millennia ago, the light spontaneously presented itself effulgent under spreading banyan trees or beyond the darkness of a cave, shattering the body, melting the mind, and revealing the spirit, only a few could find the words, could say, everything is impermanent and full of grace.

Thousands of years before time changed, in the forests of India, the *rishis* transcribed what they called "the glorious song," in the Gita, in the Vedas and Upanishads. Something more than rational recognized the All in all in the diagram for the atom within the map of the solar system sequestered at the center of each tree. The Great

Spirit sang in the rippling of a stream and the rustling leaves of the windblown trees. Memory and the mind reflected in the flames of the fire pit. Beckoned by dreams that led toward worlds yet to come in which all had slightly bewildered smiles and eyes like cornucopias of compassion, Kuan Yin sang:

"It is the song the heart was born to sing, and the mind creates itself to decipher as from the oracles of Hellenic Greece. A song awaits that creates singers like the Buddha and Black Elk, Jesus and the Magi, Mary and ourselves. As the origin of song may well have inspired the process of human evolution and taken eons to develop into the Buddha, Jesus, and Anandamayi Ma, so the development of our song parallels our personal evolution.

"Self-discovery made our songs audible, brought them to the surface so we might hear the music for ourselves. It sings the potential of the spirit. And the joy of discovery of the quality of consciousness we call the heart. It can at first be more felt than heard.

"It spreads from the center of the chest and opens the body. Clarity and joy follow the surrender as the words that express our innate wisdom rise to the tongue and become audible.

"At the edge of our universe, where fear can harden the body and doubt can turn the heart to stone, we soften the belly so the song may rise. Letting go at the edge of who we imagine we are into what we may be, we dissolve with a shudder and a sigh.

"Following a tributary from the personal to the universal, we find in our pain the pain of others as well. In our wish to be free the calling out of all who wish also to be free of the prison of themselves. Finding them in ourselves, the song that contains all sentient beings moves earth toward heaven to refresh our spiritual memory and reaffirm the work to be done."

First Singing Lesson

Last night falling asleep, the last breath could have carried me to heaven or hell and I would not have been disappointed.

This morning the universe danced before me as I sang. It loves that song.

Just behind the brow, where the frontal lobes join like hands in prayer, is the seat of creation. An altar at which to listen to the chorale of Being, the still small song within. The high ground from which we take the leap of faith.

When the heart and mind are in harmony, they produce a song. It is life calling from cell to cell.

It is a sense of our presence in the Presence. A tributary to a boundless ocean.

It is a love song, of course, which when sung changes everything.

The song echoes in the ache between the mind and the heart. The first chord grieves the lack of triumph; the last chord rejoices in it. The first burns aloud, alone on the cross of its desires. It is a penitent's prayer. The later joins in the merciful choir of forgiveness.

And when we've heard that song, know that song, against every law in heaven and earth, even that which had a beginning has no end . . .

In the song, the singer knows that anything less than this rapture is suffering. That it is the heart's longing that does all the work. He knows the ordinary mind is useless for true understanding.

When the singer stops and the song continues, you know you could hold that note forever. And you do, until at the edge of time where consciousness becomes matter, you discover the song has been singing you from the very beginning.

There is a song to be sung. A flute to be heard. Even an invisible rose.

It's not like you've forgotten completely. Some sunsets are more beautiful than others. Certain sounds resonate. Flowers still catch your eye.

There is more to it all than can be seen from our shadowy corner. It's not always easy. It takes a moment. And you never know when that moment might come!

In the meantime, sing all the songs you can until you find your own. And when you do, let it vibrate the heart-mind like a giant pipe organ in an ancient cathedral.

Let it shake loose the mullions of even our most precious and colorful concepts.

Wishful thinking leaves us wanting. But one breath at a time we can recall the song, hear the flute, smell the rose. One breath at a time we can take birth at last and complete the rondo.

When the moon becomes a coyote howl and you sleep soundly by the fire, I remember.

There is no here or there, and this and that have been a bane. In this moment, that can only be lost in the next, I hear the song. How quiet one must be—a single thought can muffle it.

And I begin to sing.

First it resonates in the vaultings of the heart, but soon it breaks free of all constraints and my song becomes the song that sings itself.

In the night, a joyous sound calls.

The little brown pygmy owl on the pinion swivels its head. The coyotes lean forward. The moon stops. As everything remembers everything in the silence between thoughts. The original song the dying sing and the birthing come to rediscover. And even Mozart couldn't sing it any better than you.

When I look into your eyes seeking my true song, a wolf looks back. Surrounding the dark center, deep amber, in which I am trapped like a Jurassic beetle. Wolf eyes drawing the formless into form. I find my throat just above my heart.

I fall in the forest and hear nothing. I am lost among the leaves and beetles. A nearly extinct salamander wanders across my nearly extinct foot.

The body makes a good sounding chamber. Whales are calling back and forth from cell to cell. The heart is full of nightingales.

We sing the same song. There is only one. It sings us too.

Saber-tooth also heard the song and never forgot it. Her golden eyes glowed. She knew she would never die.

Second Singing Lesson

A song waits from before time. It emerges from the pilgrimage of the heart.

Softening the belly so the song may rise.

Seeking the song innate we open to its unfolding.

Softening the hardness in the belly, the helplessness buried in the muscle tissue.

The tensing as if for a fall.

Softening the shielding against pain unrecognized fear floats in unexpected mercy.

Softening around holding and gradually into it I begin to melt at the edge.

Surrendering the breath into the oceanic rise and fall of the abdomen.

Levels and levels of softening.

Levels and levels of letting go.

Sensation after sensation, thought after thought dissolving in the ocean of the belly.

Following an expanding sense of Being, awareness breaches the surface whispering of the softness, then the forgiveness, which releases the song.

The armoring over the belly melting.

Rising from the ocean of the belly, we follow the breath toward the heart.

Surrendering the rigidity that holds our suffering in place.

Each breath taken directly into the heart at the center of the chest, illuminating abandoned shadows.

As something beneath the sternum begins to move.

Blessing a thousand incarnations of love and loss, the unobstructed breath passes in and out of the entrance to the heart. Opening a conduit to the song.

Third Singing Lesson

As every singer knows, we must free the breath before we can maintain a single note. Sometimes we have to clear our throat of years of confusion before we can sing. Softening the belly, we take one breath at a time. First the breath needs to ripen in the belly, then rise through the heart to expand through consciousness, clearing the throat so awareness may turn toward itself and one clear note can be heard.

Surrendering the breath, no longer holding on to it or attempting to control it, but trusting the breath to breathe on its own in the vast spaciousness of awareness, we began to learn balance in midair.

The song sings itself from the still small voice within, and we trust in not knowing what comes next.

The deeper the song, the less there is a singer or anything that separates us from the song.

The song creates a singer, not the singer creates the song.

Breaking through the fever of identification, in the joy of discovery, resonates the song.

We are what we have been looking for our whole lives.

Fourth Harmonic

When the singer lets loose the song, we no longer own our own breath.

Surrendering into the song, we drop to our knees before the Divine within. Distilled to light, it ascends past the gods and ghosts of old conditioning.

The song hangs luminous in the silver air, beckoning us past the edge of our known universe.

Letting go at the edge of who we think we are, into the joy of what we really may be, we dissolve with a shudder and a sigh.

Begun at the base of the skull, resonating through the sounding chamber of the double helix, we hear the flute that the god-drunken poet Kabir assures us will set us free. And sometimes the breath wavering through it, and if graced, the breath within that breath.

Listening a bit ecstatic, the spine like that flute, we rise an octave. There is an expectancy. Our hands rise of themselves as if to catch new worlds from birthing chants so old the rhythm remains in our pulse. The soles of the feet rippling from walking on water before we were born and during each dying. In the belly, in the center of the chest, at the top of the head, we sing ourselves.

Boundless awareness drawing us irresistibly past our edge into the song so lovely that creation stops to admire itself.

From the very origins of the song, even to the edge of the mind and beyond, there is a luminescence experienced as boundless compassion.

And we are free to live our life like a love song.

Song Without End

The last singing lesson lifts the body.

As the song echoes in the dome of the skull, it sets the fontanel ablaze.

Lighter than the thoughts on whose surface the world is mirrored, like a dream consciousness continuing into uncharted territory, expanding outward into evolution.

Rising from the top of the head, an ecstatic devotion sweeps through the universe that blesses even invisible realms.

And at the center of the song
a silence so deep
that form cannot manifest.
It is the silence which precedes
the Word.
Time and silence going beyond,
going altogether beyond gone.

Leaving all else behind, rapture follows the light. Then rests in the clear light that greets the dying and the fully born.

Listening to the song vibrating on the strands of the double helix, we take birth once again. The tides of new-born stars and disintegrating moons flooding the universe of each cell.

And where we expected to encounter the singer, we find only the idea of a singer.

Nothing we have learned is of any use because there is nothing to control.

The song's origins reveal the bottomland of the ground of being.

The wild wisdom of the song's lyrics converges from ten directions. Unencumbered by reason it discloses how even suffering fits perfectly into the scheme of things. Beyond pleasure and pain, we see how our attachment to each attracts incarnations from across time. Entering our true grace, the origin of the song. There is nowhere else to go. Nothing else to be. No truth greater than knowing rests in being.

Beyond that, only love survives.

In the after-hum of our true song, blessings arise that are too beautiful for words.

After having given the teachings on the origin of our original song, sitting on a great stone outcropping, Kuan Yin sang to the sea dragons that guarded her sacred island, humming the birth of Buddhas while the sea dragons rose to the surface to pay their respects.

She bows to the rising up; calling forth the great waters, the beneficent dragons swim to her side. Developing an eternal relationship with the supplicant South Sea dragons that gather for her blessing.

She was also known as the Mother of All the Oceans of the Heart and Mind for attending to the waves of the South China Sea and the fishermen on them. And for protecting all those riding the waves in meditation rising and falling on the ocean of being. A protector of the dharma, inspiring humanity to observe the winds from all directions that can blow the mind off course. She protects the pilgrims crossing to the other shore. The dragons of mindfulness "biting through" the moorings of attachment.

Chapter 9

KUAN YIN AND THE DRAGONS

The etymology of the word "dragon" is similar to that of the mindfulness practice *vipassana*, which means "to see clearly."

The evolutionary predecessor of the dragon is the naga. The synapse jumped, echoing the leap of faith from slithering lizard to flying bird, a release of the primal energy that breaks free from formlessness into form. The big bang of Being into beingness.

The dragon does not, as legend would have it, prefer to have its nest in China. It resides at the base of the spine as evolution.

In the course of evolution, as reptiles evolved into birds, not only could they fly, but they began to dream. In that (r)evolutionary leap of consciousness, the brightening light of awareness dispelled many of the shadows that passed for reality, providing insight into the nature of consciousness and the spirit.

The dragon, perhaps the missing link between planes of reality, representing too the evolution from lizard to bird, appears in the interstice between levels of being. A shamanic steed.

Dragon Mother says it is as true to say she exists as to say she doesn't; she would not quarrel with either. Being as much the vastness between the seeming solidity of thoughts as the swirling *maya* ("illusion") of thought itself, she does not take sides but suggests mercy where friction might arise.

The interstitial dragon, a missing link somewhere between Quetzalcoatl and pterodactyl, a cosmic amphibian meeting on the cosmic bridge, the corpus callosum connecting heaven and earth. Poised like Kuan Yin in midair

where the healer invites the healing, removing the obstacles to the heart, she makes room for the sacred.

In Asian cultures the dragon often represents eternity—or, deeper yet, timelessness, and the deciphering of the senses. In Central America, Quetzalcoatl, the plumed serpent, personifies this momentous transformation from the earth element to the air element.

The dragon is a "leak-through" from other planes on which is sung the Origin of Song. The dragon that followed us home from school one day to put an end to time and unholy confusion.

The sea dragons so infused with the compassion of Kuan Yin became an image of blessing to the collective consciousness of Asia.

It is rumored that their flying cousins, having been greeted at the other end of the Silk Road with curses and violence, instead of reverence and praise, were moody and cantankerous.

Unfortunately for the flying dragons, their intentions were wholly misunderstood and they were hunted by the near-sighted who knew little of innate beneficence and mistook them for the serpent in Eden.

The dragons want the world to know they did not offer the apple in the garden. They only taught that there is no death, and that the world is a dream. Only said: The world needs to become real in your heart for the healing to begin. Just love each other as you might yourself. If you can forgive yourself, you can forgive anyone.

The ocean-going, sea-loving dragon, greeted at first with the awe that often precedes insight, was pure spirit, like many of our unknown and unrecognized gifts that have the power to liberate. Noting there are many realities, none of which is any more real than another.

When did flight and dream combine in that first rhythmic line that chanted in birth and eased our death? When did the first poem that warmed the blood rise from the heart as travelogue for the wandering mind?

And when, in the aerodynamics of that flying spirit, did we become aware we were aware? Singing at the edge of the known, an evolutionary leaning toward compassion.

Chapter 10

THE SORROW OF THE DRAGON KING

From her years on Mount Putuo, Kuan Yin shared a long history with beneficent dragons.

There is an old story of a great Dragon King who lost his two sons. Having disguised themselves as carp in order to frolic about in the sea, darting and tumbling through the waves, the brothers fell afoul of an old fisherman's net. Hauled aboard, out of the waters necessary for them to return to their original form, they were destined for the day's fresh fish market.

But the fisherman noticed the two exceptionally well-proportioned fish were quite unique as they kept breathing after being taken aboard. He imagined they were some sort of magical creatures whose flesh might have healing powers, even a magical curative for illness, and would certainly draw a crowd to his stall and perhaps even be auctioned to curious buyers. This was his lucky day!

Because his sons were gone, the Dragon King had no one to ask for help in retrieving his miscreant offspring who might soon suffer dismemberment and death. And if they were recognized as magical beings, particularly dragons, they would be imprisoned and slowly mutilated to expose the source of their powers.

The Dragon King, bereft and weeping, knew nowhere to turn. Who could help his sons and all the sons lost to their parents, surrounded by misery?

Kuan Yin heard the Dragon King's cries and brought to his attention Shan Tsai, the disabled servant boy the Dragon King had raised from birth, whose one shortened leg left him with a noticeable limp. The king beseeched the boy to take what little money was on hand, go to the market, and buy back his wayward sons before they were cut up and parceled out to the long line of buyers shaking their money above their heads, anxious to take some magic home. The boy was unsure what to do, but he so loved the king that he went forth, uncertain if he would even survive to return.

The market was an unknown world. Shan Tsai had never seen such a conglomeration of twisting energy. No place for a lost child difficult to find among the lost souls who jostled and argued, never recognizing the magic before them or within them. Everyone blindly struggling for a happiness that was only to be found within. There was nothing of the kindness he had been nurtured by. He wondered if he was in hell. A place for lost souls cut off from their sacred center. It was terrifying and dangerous, the buyers' grief replacing the marrow in their bones,

their pain sequestered at the base of the skull. Anything could happen.

At the market, what little money Shan Tsai had quickly proved insufficient against the bids of the anxious mob. He could feel his dragon father grieving back in his grotto where he might remain to mourn the rest of his life.

Not feeling he had any alternative, the boy heroically interposed himself in front of the first angry buyer and revealed to the old fisherman, who would be able to profit so greatly from his catch, the true identity of the fish-seeming dragon boys and told him that though the fisherman might lose a great bounty, the Dragon King would lose even more.

And he begged the fisherman to stop for a moment, turn toward his heart, and listen in a moment's stillness to the dragon father weeping with a helplessness and loss that echoed all the losses of the world the old man too had experienced. And the mariner, unwilling to cause such suffering even at his own expense, secreted the wayward fish in a basket and sent them home to their father.

His sons saved by Kuan Yin, the Dragon King's gratitude was so great, he sent to the suffering world his granddaughter, Lung Nu, who held the bright-shining flaming pearl, whose illumination was the gift of awareness to humankind. Coming to attend to those in need with the same dedication to kindness as the fisherman's, Long Nu nurtured those committed to mercy and service to all sentient beings.

Becoming Kuan Yin

And when the selfless fisherman was invited into the great hall of the Dragon King, his heart expanded so from the element of compassion that he could hardly breathe. Filled with Kuan Yin's all-abiding generosity, he pledged himself to feed the hungry, and each day he brought heaps of fresh fish to the impoverished village at the far end of the harbor.

You may have noticed that many Chinese dragons play with a ball of light known as the sacred pearl; this is thought to be the source of their power.

The ball of light, the pearl of luminous awareness, and the dragon of compassion are often found in close proximity at serious play. An icon rising from the under-dream (the mental collectivity below the level of awareness), the dragon represents the ancient spirit power in the spine. The pearl of awareness, the chi that, rising through the water-born, fire-breathing spine, produces the dawn of awakening.

Chapter 11

MANY BUDDHAS

Meditating on the peak of Mount Putuo, Kuan Yin met a wizened old monk—or mountain spirit—sitting in front of a deep cave. Watching her approach, he raised a water bladder and offered her a cup to quiet her thirst.

Appreciating such a hospitable gesture, she sat next to the old hermit and asked how long he had been living in this place. The monk said he could no longer remember but that he had long become at home sharing his cave with "red, eons-old spirit-bears," which he said were the earliest incarnations of the earliest Buddhas.

Kuan Yin had always had a special reverence for bears, which she could not quite explain.

The aged monk said, "Gautama often spoke of being only the latest of thousands of Buddhas, that he related in particular to Dipankara, his twenty-fourth predecessor, which, because of the great distances of time before another emanation appeared, could even have been a

Neanderthal wise man, shaman, or great mother, before language could recall them.

"Since Buddha-nature is our first ancestor, why couldn't it have arisen, before time was devised, in any creature humanoid or earlier, occurring when need arose?"

Taking her into the cave, the monk showed Kuan Yin three ancient skulls, each with an ochre circle on its crown. A Neolithic remnant of the Jataka bear's origins of the practice of kindness and compassion.

And they sat together until she knew the names of these earliest spirit seekers. And continued to call them by name when as Mother of All Wildings she entered into the healing circle.

The monk said he thought maybe this great cave bear whose heart-mind was completely open may have been the source of the legend among the native peoples of the Yellow Valley who met a spirit who roamed the forest, occasionally transmitting healings, burial rituals, and shared silences with those whose love was greater than their fear. Taking the beholders "past the edge of the world" on the leafy path beyond time or change.

Closing her eyes, Kuan Yin rested in being. The sun passing slowly through the om, the first monotheism, vibrating in the atmosphere as lightning strikes the primal seas and shocks life into existence.

The keen-eyed green heron, the sparrow's lilting the warp and woof of the living tapestry. Cattails bursting cotton-winged syllables into an epic haiku, *Swaha!*

The sun hangs blue vines from thousand-year-long cypresses. The golden stream bathing green moss, black river stones stippled with silver dew.

Rolling west across ocean meadows, the sun revives the archives of the earth where fossil pollens drift from extinct plants. Doves and starlings decorate the pinion forests scattering hulls like rose pedals at a wedding.

Crows, the spirit messengers, mark the rebirth far from Lhasa.

Like prayer flags, ravens on the wind rising up from the forest floor. Large black birds with blessing yellow eyes potlatching with the human spirit, causing the heart and mind to reunite.

What a wonderful place, she thought, to sit quietly forever.

Chapter 12

HEALING IN
OUR DREAMS

When Kuan Yin left her body behind and became a dream, she could be everywhere at once and bless people in their sleep, riding the shape-shifting dragon of compassion on imagistic beta waves.

Kuan Yin takes us under her arm, whispering in our ear or appearing in our dreams to display to us what the next initiation might be.

When as a child Miao Shan overheard the recitation of a passing sage about the power of mercy and loving-kindness to heal the ills of the world, she fell into a deep sleep, receiving teachings in her dreams that continued for years. From this lineage of dream transmissions, she became known to employ that manner of wisdom transference for eons.

As Kuan Yin has freed the demons from hell and released the suffering of the gods and Titans, so in her unlimited mercy she comes as compassion to lighten the dark end of existence.

Compassion comes to test us in our dreams, to incite sudden wordless understandings that cross one frontier after another.

Some dreams open what seems to be the Book of Wisdom. We wake feeling as though we may have received teachings from the Ascended Masters. Whatever happens when dreams arise more from the heart's mind than the mechanical brain's, a greater participation in the universal can often be noted. We arise feeling as though we have read a remarkable spiritual work. We awake ecstatic.

When such a truth-teller comes to visit us in our dreams, there is nowhere to hide. She is calling out all us miserable, unsuccessful controllers of our slippery fate. She tells us no old trick will protect us, that only surrender to the miracle of compassion can set us free.

These are blessing dreams. Pull yourself to the side of your bed and sit quietly. Secure this teaching in the heart. Don't be too rational. Was it real?

This breaking through of the boundary between the dream world and "waking reality"—long acknowledged by spiritual adepts as actually a continuation of the same realm—expanded both Kuan Yin's frame of reference and the planes from which the cries of distress could be heard. She took us in her dreams to other worlds to illuminate what we barely comprehend, how compassion is the active element of wisdom, the quality the sages and pundits ejected from heaven realms needed to cultivate. She was the soother of ghosts and the healer of displaced souls.

Kuan Yin comes on the fluttering wings of REM (dream uncovering) to unveil the path that compassion recommends. In dreamtime, the Presence in presence reveals itself. Other realities present themselves.

Sometimes this momentary clarity of vision discloses how close we may be getting to being reborn just on the other side of our fear.

Sometimes her unpredictable compassion comes to us in our sleep to show us how much mercy it takes to live in this frightening world. How the hindrances are vulnerable to reconditioning; how the tangle just beneath the surface is susceptible to courage and loving care. How deep investigation may unravel, and spiritual experiences access the heart where our liberation awaits.

Sometimes compassion comes as a large jungle cat that initiates us, as she does so many, if only we can stay awake after we wake up. Sometimes the beasts that test us are not otherworldly but remnants of our childhood night terrors, projections from the familiar unknown whose big yellow eyes stare out at us from an impenetrable thicket. Some of these dreams unite us with another world we have dared not consider.

Kuan Yin once appeared to Tian, one of her chosen emissaries, as a panther in his dreams to take him to the next level. Tian, whose full story will be told in a later book, *In the Time of the Smiling Buddhas,* was led to go beyond himself to save the world, to protect the earth mysteries, the deep teachings in plain sight, when the eye

of beauty opens and we discover the marvel of traditional landscape painting. Moving the viewer to preserve the spirit still living in the mountains and rivers.

Tian wrote of seeing Kuan Yin appear as a wildcat in his dreams:

> The first night a black panther casually crosses the room. But before I can even think of escape, the big cat leaves and returns with two tawny mountain lions who just sit and watch.
>
> The following night a steel-gray mountain lion is sitting in the garden, her long, gray tail draped like a Japa mala about a white marble Buddha's shoulders. In her eyes, black vortices lead to panther paradise on a quiet ledge above

a vast forest. As dreamer, I did not wish to be any-where else.

In the morning I wondered if perhaps such marvelous apparitions were always present but just unseen. And I wondered if perhaps I was just dream-seeing what I was normally blind to.

There was nowhere to go, but before the fear could take hold, a feeling arose that they had come to remove the fear from my eyes. But I didn't quite trust myself to be sure that was their purpose.

As Kuan Yin continued her nightly visitations now without the mountain lions, I began to look forward to her presence even though when she first appeared each night, it took me a moment to be at ease. One night she didn't show up, and I wondered if she was all right. It was odd to be concerned with the well-being of an object of my fear.

The next night she reappeared in a lush meadow beside a small stream. She and I, ly-ing near each other, listened together for what seemed hours to the water gently flowing. We may have even entered each other's sensory field, she hearing as I might and I flicking my pointed ears at each changing trickle. I experienced through her how much more she heard of the chiming in the water than did my normal diminished sensory field. She seemed to feel sad for my partial deafness.

Her world was much larger than mine. And through this crossing-over of the species barrier, I experienced an otherwordly sense of familiarity and trust. Whatever was happening in these moments of interbeing changed the size of the world I lived in.

My next sleep finds me in an open meditation lodge in a clearing surrounded by verdant jungle. I can hear the ocean, smell the waves beyond the dense thicket. I am eating rice and seaweed. Half finished, I leave my bowl, drawn by a path that disappears into the trees. Following the trail between dense foliage, I come upon a clearing.

At the far end of the open ground are two enormous tigers perhaps seven hundred pounds each. Heads down, they slowly approach. My gut turns as they draw near, but it is not a fight-or-flight response but instead the trembling that precedes revelation. Weak-kneed on the verge of the Divine, I drop to my knees and began to weep. I cannot contain the wonderment.

The golden cats come forward with the familiarity of a brood-mate. They wrap themselves around my legs and graze me with tongues smooth as silk. Ecstasy sweeps over me as our worlds enfold. When I return from the clearing to the restaurant, there on the table where I left it is my bowl still warm and ready to be consumed.

In the last series of dream meetings I noticed that the tigers had a somewhat unusual coloring: a maroon stripe between the usual yellow, black, and white markings.

The usual fear would arise for just a moment upon seeing them again and then quickly disappear as they approached, but this time one came right up to my face and, looking straight into my eyes, opened wide its mouth. I knew what was to be done. I laid my head inside his cavernous jaws onto the rough red pillow of his tongue. I am not sure what happened next, perhaps my mind stopped between thoughts, but I had a feeling of being loved and of loving as I had never known.

Between this dream and those that followed, in which I always ended up putting my head in the tiger's mouth, I recognized the maroon stripe was the Tibetan maroon of my first teacher's robes who opened me to Kuan Yin and stole my heart years before.

Putting my head in the tiger's mouth was to commit all it takes to get ourselves free and to share what is awoken for the benefit of others, including all that is known and unknown in the continual uncovering of our inherent wisdom and compassion.

It is a series of dreams that must be had, and may arise even in advanced stages of growth as a benign remembrance of the work to be done before the next step forward.

These compassionate dreams come to destroy our defenses and bring us to our knees to discover the humility the heart requires to go on. They illuminate our youthful and not-so-youthful folderol—the misdoings, missed moments, unkindness, and indifference to the pain of others, and, oddly, our attachment to our own. They wake us in a cold sweat, praying for the kindness we may have denied another. Our tears will not dissuade her from revealing the true meaning of forgiveness even when forgiveness is nearly impossible.

Compassion's fierce determination to help us overcome our mercilessness to others and ourselves asks, would you rather break that momentum now, or on your deathbed?

Her almost unbearable compassion is the chance of a lifetime. These terrible/wonderful dreams are part of the healing we took birth for. She uses the opportunity of our dreams to turn our fears to grace, to teach us steadfastness and surrender.

Some bad dreams come just in time to save us. Getting our attention, they focus us on the hindrances to clarity. They clarify the thought stream and straighten twisted intentions. They are the slayers of thousands, of millions, of pain-inducing thoughts and feelings. Their strongest medicine is remembrance. They bring Kuan Yin to mind.

Kuan Yin, in her guise as the eater of impurities, devours all that remains unloved for an evening snack and infuses the wound with loving-kindness. As she did for Tian, she devours our karma and leaves the heart's larder full.

In Maitreya's medicine bag are frightful healing dreams that can demonstrate what the world would be without love. We awake with tears rolling down our faces and an increased will to serve.

I wonder if some of these healing dreams might originate from bodhisattvas who committed between lives to aid the dazed passing through to find a more advantageous rebirth. And so too creating bridges—the teacher Nisargadatta Maharaj speaks of the mind creating the abyss and the heart crossing it—traversing the interstice between worlds in our dreams.

Sometimes Kuan Yin employs fierce protective spirits to protect "the dream that dreams" from being seduced by fear. These spirits are not vengeful, just fierce; the destroyers of ignorance, the personifications of insistent compassion. They are the guardians at the edge of the pit who call us back from falling. They bind the wounds of our wrath.

She says, "Give it to me." And without preamble or excuse, the penitent divulge the blockages to freedom and perhaps open those words never uttered before, hidden in their hearts.

Giving up our back-breaking attachment to our suffering, bent too long under the weight of shame and self-rejection, this affliction-devouring night visitor offers the rare opportunity to "put your head in the lion's mouth" once and for all, to surrender your suffering into the lion's roar of the Original Heart. And pass that mercy on to others.

When the frightful eater comes for a midnight snack, give him the worst you have to offer. And let the wave of compassion carry you into the shared heart.

She says, "Let your practice be devotion to the state of compassion. Love not as a state of mind but as a quality of Being."

Chapter 13

FOR PAIN'S
SAKE

Kuan Yin represents the skillful means that opens our heart to our suffering. Letting go of everything that keeps us small, we find the words that can forgive us for being in so much pain. Forgetting and remembering, falling from moment to moment, we learn balance in midair.

We have a mean habit of sending hatred into our pain, transforming it to suffering just when it is calling most for mercy. We harden to others' pain as well. It is that pain, more often than not, by which we define ourselves. But there is a song that remembers love no matter how difficult. No longer mesmerized by our wounds, we stop running for our lives. Slowly in the shifting silences of meditation, in the momentary quietude between breaths, from a quavering voice within, we begin the song that changes everything.

Kuan Yin suggests developing a merciful consciousness and sending loving-kindness, even forgiveness, into our pain rather than judging it as a punishment or a curse.

Taking our judgment off the cross to embrace our pain instead of further rejecting it and condensing it to suffering. Forgiving ourselves for being, even involuntarily, in so much pain. Sometimes it takes a lot of mercy to counterbalance the absurd self-flagellation of the mind. Cultivating a merciful consciousness of that which suffering endures and the compassion necessary to equalize the imbalance.

Easing the resistance to unwanted input before it bursts into flame, we practice these teachings of Kuan Yin as we would with lighter weights in the gymnasium of discomfort.

Because we are one of those sentient beings, we have vowed to liberate, confronting the wrathful deities of our resistance that surround our pain is an important initiation.

It is said that nothing is true until we have experienced it, so as an experiment in sending healing into an area where fear has displaced acceptance, we use the occasion of moderate pain to test the truth of softening and the power of mercy to cultivate a lifeline to healing.

As an experiment in compassion and the cultivation of mercy, one might consider focusing one's attention on a slight wound or burn, softening about it and sending loving-kindness into the injury. Note any thought hindrances that arise to limit such an exercise. These are the wrathful deities in angel's garb misguiding us to defend ourselves against such absurd ideas as sending love into pain. The wrong-headed guardians of our pain that maintain helplessness and hopelessness, isolating discomfort from the sympathetic incursion of a healing mercy.

Notice the changes that go on in the synaptic field, softening, releasing the tightening, breathing mercy into the pain, opening the conduit to the heart, making us wonder how love turned up in a place like this!

Comparing the healing of an injury into which mercy was sent with a similar one left to its own devices, which healed faster?

Approaching the calcified ring of resistance around our pain, which limits the penetration of healing, we soften to the fear that congregates around difficulty. Releasing the tightening that intensifies pain before it recedes further into its suffering.

Softening reveals our inherent capacity for mercy, the very personal relief from the teachings in compassion.

The heart whispers, "May I get the most out of this possible. May we be freed from the grasping around our pain as mercy gradually infiltrates our pain?"

Recognizing that this working with physical pain parallels the healing of mental discomfort, we release the tension (aversion/resistance) around such fulminations, softening from the edge inward. Trust and patience blossoming in our merciful consciousness. Courage entering further.

Softening is a physical trigger for the mental state of letting go.

We cultivate this softening in the belly in the moment-to-moment letting go of what hinders the heart. When fear, pride, or doubt, aversion or anger, reflections of a lifetime of holding arise in a merciful consciousness, it mindfully and heartfully watches these afflictive thoughts dissipate into the eternity from which they came.

The next time you stub your toe, instead of sending the habitual aversion that so mimics hatred into the already agitated sensations, consider love.

As the pain is cut loose from its habitual moorings, this opening around pain has been shown to increase the flow of the immune system to the affected area. Because we are conditioned to send hatred into our pain, when we let go of our negative attachment to what ails us, this compulsive resistance, and instead send love where it was never considered possible, we turn the tables on our loathing.

Healing is to reoccupy those parts of ourselves abandoned to pain; to enter with mercy and awareness those areas withdrawn from in fear.

Experimenting, as suggested, with a minor cut or burn, we see how an area softened around and used as a focus for loving-kindness may heal days before another that is turned away from. Compare the time it might take a wound met with mercy to heal to one that is not.

Working with our pain is an act of compassion to others as well, allowing us to stay a bit longer at the bedside of one frightened or agonized by birth and dying. Allowing us to keep our heart open in hell.

When the compassion we send into our pain begins to include others experiencing this same pain at the same time, a "reversal of fortune" occurs as we experience not just our own pain but *the* pain, the shared pain that inhabits the common body. No longer your problem alone, the pain we all share creates a community of interbeing and healing. *My* pain is a tragedy; *the* pain is a further teaching in compassion. When we meet pain with mercy, we serve a world of suffering.

The Healing in the Wound

Those we have worked with who have sent whatever mercy they could muster into even something small, such as an open wound, a bad scrape, or a burn, have found a measurable lessening in infection and a quickening in healing. A growing concern for not just their pain but *the* pain.

Our natural resistance to pain, physical and mental, in the mind, seems to offer the heart a chance to be free. It is a gift that keeps on giving. A growing connection with all those others who too may feel a loss of grace. Who long for some surcease of sorrow. A concern not just for my pain but for all pain.

A gift of healing that grows in the heart of every injury. The shared pain of not just my wound but the wound, which attunes us to the heart of another. And intensifies our ability to relate to our pain instead of solely from it. Offering a spaciousness from which we could begin to respond rather than compulsively react to so many other difficult moments in life. Sharing in the "birth pangs" of us all as we come back into a world calling for mercy and awareness, completing our own birth.

Overcoming the mean-spirited habit of sending anger and even hatred into our pain just when it is calling out most for mercy. Reminding us of the unwanted circumstances we all share, and as the wise recommend, to treat pain as if it were in our only child. Before it contracts around the heart, turning our pain to suffering.

The gift in the wound makes us more mindful of how little love we send into our suffering. Or the difficulties of others. It wakes us up. A return to the heart-mind that moves toward difficulties rather than turns away from them, allowing the entrance of mindfulness and mercy into the wound. This is as true for a cut or tumor as it is the sense of disappointment in the mind.

Realizing how little our feet have touched the ground. An increased capacity to listen to ourselves with a merciful ear, to turn to ourselves and others as if we are our only child and meet pain, discomfort, even cold loneliness, with a merciful awareness. Once awoken, mercy has a healing way of its own.

To touch with mercy that which we have withdrawn from in fear is strong medicine. Instead of turning pain to suffering, we deal directly to the mind and body from the heart. Softening around the unpleasant, noting the tendency of fear to project nasty futures. Instead returning as often as possible to the moment-to-moment process of releasing the hardness that accumulates around the wound. Surrendering to the possibility of healing.

This gift of mercy sent into our pain as well as others', opening the tension around the injury, increasing access to the immune system, brings healing at many levels. Opening the fist cramped around the frightened body and mind cultivates kindness for all the weary beings living in the pain we share.

The more we forgive our own pain we are in, the more generosity flows to others and is reflected back as an increased capacity for happiness and even love.

Directing forgiveness, a habit of loving-kindness, to that which distracts us from our True Heart. Awaking each morning with mercy in the breath. Expanding the circle, which includes all those experiencing this same pain in this same body-mind, dry-birthed on the shores of the ocean of compassion.

The gift that can re-hearten so many levels of unhappiness and open a more suitable life at the heart of life. Levels and levels of softening, levels and levels of letting go of the pained contents of the small mind opening into the big Mind enormity of being.

Chapter 14

THE BELLY OF COMPASSION

Bring your attention into the sensation in the body. Just feel what sits here. Feel this body you were born into. Allow awareness to come to the level of sensation in the body.

Gradually allow your attention to drop into the abdomen. And begin to soften to the sensations in the belly. Softening the belly to receive the breath. Softening the belly to receive life. Softening to any resistance. No holding. No grasping in soft belly.

Letting go of the hardness in the belly. Practicing "merciful belly."

Moment to moment softening the belly. Moment to moment making room for your life.

Don't try to grasp or trap the breath, to shape or control it. Just let it be.

Surrender to the breath, softening the belly from moment to moment.

In soft belly is the release of the posturing of a lifetime. All the grief hidden hard in the belly. Have mercy. Letting the hardness float in soft belly.

Levels and levels of softening. Levels and levels of letting go. Levels and levels of letting be.

The belly fatigued with its holding, with its mercilessness to itself. Have mercy. Just for this moment at least, soften to this ancient clinging. In a new mercy. In a new willingness to heal. Have mercy on this mercilessness.

Each in breath, belly rising. Each exhalation, belly falling. Rising and falling, let your breath breathe itself. Letting go of control, trust the breath to breathe all by itself.

Each breath breathing itself in soft belly. In soft belly we have room for it all. Even room for our pain. Room to get born, room even to die in soft belly, in merciful belly.

Levels and levels of softening. Levels and levels of letting go.

Reinhabit the body that has existed more as a thought than a reality until pain catches our attention and gives it back to us, battered and wounded, or catch a glimpse of it reflected in a dysmorphic mirror or a desire-filled store window. Momentary pleasure a lasting pain, momentary pain if an object in big Mind overcomes the tendency to contract, a pain that can end suffering when received in a merciful awareness that can become a "gift in the wound"

from which we receive an increase in our capacity for insight and compassion.

The gift is a sense in the midst of our pain of the thousands of others also sharing this difficulty. An opportunity to see *the* pain in *my* pain. A change in states of mind that softens the body and relieves the mind. Extending kindness to those sharing this same pain takes a leap of mercy and joins us in the community of healing, the healing we took birth for. A growing connection with all those others who too may feel a loss of grace. Who long for some surcease of sorrow.

A gift of healing that grows in the heart of every injury. The shared heart that attunes us to the heart of another.

Chapter 15

PURE LAND

In Buddha's later teachings, Kuan Yin rose from within the Lotus Sutra. She stood at the entrance to the real dream of a land of pure practice, a wisdom abode in which it was hoped one might continue the spiritual practices begun during their lifetime under circumstances reminiscent of celestial realms. She teaches that when one's heart turns that Pure Land can be seen.

To some this may sound suspiciously similar to the Judeo-Christian heavens and hells of the personally unsatisfying religious upbringing they turned away from to undertake the investigation of their Buddha-nature. However, these "astral" realms, seemingly bordering on the mythological, are open to exploration in depth meditation. Noting the underlying wishful thinking that might project hopeful mirages on the back of the skull, we do not jump to any conclusions, but knowing the power of spiritual practice, we see the value of a merciful consciousness for the sake of all.

Practicing seeing hearing tasting touching feeling and thinking as though it were real, while knowing it only seems that way; recognizing there are planes where one knows better, I reside on this impetuous plane practicing awakening. I reside in this temporary body in order to find the Presence in presence. What else is one to do?

As an experiment in the devotional surrender, which had at times carried me beyond the relative and rational into the undifferentiated spaciousness of Being the mind experiences as effusive love, I asked Kuan Yin to reveal to me, as far as I might comprehend, the "reality" of Pure Land.

Perhaps because each mindful breath is another step on the path, Kuan Yin directed me to "fall into my breath."

As the mind stilled and sank like a bright bubble down through the sea, it did not stop at the ocean bottom but continued right through "the floor of the mind." There was no one in control.

All I thought or felt, saw or heard, was not my own, but floated on the idea of me. I was essentially just aware-ness observing. From the perspective of "just awareness," watching thoughts, ideas, perceptions come into being and disappear on the shroud of some equally imagined thinker, all I identified with as "me" was like a dream dreamed by a dream. At the heart of self-extant awareness, free from such entanglement, settled away from all these habitual trinkets—the "call and response" of the senses— in that absolute stillness rarely perceived on the surface, there existed beyond the world of name and form what might easily be called a Pure Land. The luminosity of absolute vastness which, it is reputed, the spiritual heroes, the bodhisattvas and hardy adherents to their practice, pass through and can analogously manifest wherever need calls them, under the aegis of a heart liberated from self-interest for the benefit of others for incarnations to come.

It became clear that this Pure Land is not elsewhere, nor is it acquired by the acquisition of some spiritual "merit," but by the balance of mind and heart that allows us to stand on the ground of being, experiencing the clarity and joy of our inherent nature. The Zen patriarch Huineng points out that the accumulation of merit with the attachment to some outcome beneficial to the "collector" can drag us to realms quite other than a Pure Land.

Merit is not "brownie points" that put us on some waiting list. Merit is the uncovering of insight into our true nature. Increasing clarity of mind. Wisdom teachings in our dreams; silent, wordless understandings that refine our love. Merit is the activation of the Pure Land of our unconditional heart. If we look for our heart outside ourselves, we miss the gathering by death of peripheral thoughts and sensations into the clear light of the True Heart.

Pure Land was not, as some teachings may assert, only a "place" we might go after we die, but a frame of reference in the living present. More than a state of mind, a state of being, noted perhaps particularly in meditation, or in an aha moment whose origins have been debated through millennia. A seeing through the superficiality of phenomena to the luminous kernel of truth at the center.

Which of course does not mean, particularly on the path with a heart, disregarding or diminishing the importance of such relative phenomena. For it is on that peripheral plane that we live most of our lives and the ability to embrace suffering is most needed. And the capacity to serve is most required.

The devotional quality that had occasionally taken me beyond myself became a tool for my not knowing and simply trusting where Kuan Yin was drawing me. Pure Land as the environment for our luminous nature, the incandescent heart of our inherent wisdom and compassion.

Seeking the unimaginable, incomparable truth in the shadows it casts at the back of our head, we yet, remarkably through some indefinable grace, get it right sometimes.

When I asked one of my oldest teachers what Pure Land meant to him, he said, "Infinity, where bodhisattvas become Buddhas and then bodhisattvas."

Becoming Kuan Yin

Chapter 16

THE EMISSARIES
OF COMPASSION

Kuan Yin is often seen in the company of her two aco-
lytes, emissaries of compassion who appear to so many in
so many forms, from teachers to dream animals.

It may be noticed in later depictions of Kuan Yin that
on one side of her stands Shan Tsai who, imbued with
the energy of the bodhisattva's vow, became her blessed
attendant. On her other side, of course, is Long Nu, the
Dragon Maiden, dressed like Kuan Yin in a plain shawl,
who holds a giant orb called the night brilliance pearl, or
for some, the pearl of great price, emitting an illumination
of humankind, the enormous light of awareness. These
celestial guardian attendants, who, according to anecdotal
evidence, act as emissaries of Kuan Yin's cause, are often
sent to bring mercy to the lost and frightened.

Kuan Yin chose her emissaries to integrate the full-
blown heart into the struggling mind. Her fulfilled emissaries appear as the Dharma in different forms at different
times. Sometimes as the turning words of loved ones, or

a whisper outside the window we are opening. Books fall open to remind us. A teaching beyond us at an earlier time offers a forgotten gift. Mercy streams past suffering into the pain that ends pain. Met by love instead of flat-minded fear, closure, or isolation in "my pain," it opens into that same pain shared by thousands, perhaps millions, an empathy for all in this same condition. In our cries, she hears the cries of all.

Or some say as a specter that leads the lost to safety, much like "angelic Bernice's voice" in the First World War. A whisper in the desperate ear; a vision of a divine personage that reminds us of our sacred essence. Such emissaries initiate the shamans and give her her healing song and the power of transmission that will expand the heart and mind of those who wish nothing more.

Many are bodhisattvas-in-training, healers, peacemakers, servers of those getting balanced and light. Living simply by the code of common decency. They invest the dharma into those likely to love clearly.

They are devoted to the path of healing. Repairing the hearts and mending the minds of those able to hear the turning word. Or restoring the earth tones to the shallows of the mind and preserving the perfections of nature, as Tian does.

All those in whom kindness and consciousness grow, devoted to self-discovery, who in healing themselves tend to heal much about them.

On the bodhisattva path, there are many different travelers, various right-minded adherents attempting to follow the path. They are the vow-takers whose goal is the liberation of themselves and others. Those who have committed themselves to live mindfully and heartfully for the benefit of others for as long as they live.

They are those standing on either side of us because they will not sit until their work is done. Those who have vowed to actualize their inborn potential in the meditation hall or chapel, in the family room or lookout tower.

They are the peacekeepers, the heartful teachers, the earth protectors, the healers and gardeners of Buddhanature, budding bodhisattvas who, like Arjuna in the Bhagavad Gita, stand between opposing factions attempting to calm the ten thousand inclinations to grasp and attack of those who cannot yet see, by cultivating in the no-man's-land between thoughts, between beats of the heart, the tendency to share love. Those who open-handedly offer loving-kindness with whatever spiritual strength is available. The menders of the wound, these hidden healers and peacemakers offer hidden words during the day and turning words in our dreams.

They are pilgrims who manifest the simplest of truths. That service to all sentient beings is not a manifestation of enlightenment but simply the path that mimics our inherent compassion.

Chapter 17

LONG NU

Long Nu knew the moment she met Kuan Yin that this was her teacher and became spontaneously enlightened. This is the first mention in Buddhist literature of instant enlightenment, of a flower bursting into full bloom in midair—no bo tree, no arduous precepts, no winter, no summer; just spring, just the open arms of undifferentiated compassion. It is as well the first mention of a woman so blessed.

Kuan Yin told her, "Now that you know me, you know that healing precedes cure. Love is the deepest form of acceptance. The limitless possibilities of the shared heart to reach out in sympathetic joy to another. It is through pure speech, medicine words, that you will reach into the hearts of those longing to be free.

"Most attracted to the spirit are drawn by a great loneliness. A longing for completion. They cannot understand why they perhaps began life in something of a hell not realizing that was the first necessary step on the path to fruition.

"The heart must sometimes be broken open to make room for one's full potential. It is the pain that ends our pain, and embraces others to soothe their suffering. It is the nature of this terrible and wonderful world into which you were born to find the miraculous.

"Do you think it was otherwise for Miao Shan in the blood-stained palace, the foul drudgery of the nunnery, the wailing demons in hell? How else would I have found the dharma, the priceless jewel of *Om mani padme hum* that brought me through to the Pure Land stillness of fully letting go, the great release of suffering, the formula of the Prajna Paramita Heart Sutra that lets go of anything but unconditional love, of anything that obscures the fullness of Being?

"When these wisdom teachings are integrated, there is room to breathe in the pure compassion of her great mantra: *Gate, gate, paragate, parasamgate, bodhi swaha!*, which leads to the obliteration of the hindrances to our original grace: 'Gone, gone, gone beyond, gone altogether beyond, nothing but clarity remains!'

"The primal healing of the origin of song is yours to give as an emissary of my benevolence."

Thereafter those who came to Long Nu in need found themselves looking into their original face.

Now enlightened, Long Nu asked, "To whom should I now pray?" To which Kuan Yin replied, "Pray to the mercy that holds one heart to another, to the love that attracts kindness, the generosity that serves the needy, the forgiveness that brings the lonely to the dharma, the compassion that motivates the formless."

As part of her healer's training, Kuan Yin imparted to Long Nu the technique of "the turning word" that turns one toward realization:

"Poetry is a shortcut to the subconscious. It finds the words to express the inexpressible. It calls intuition to the surface, revealing a deeper self. It is fluent in love and the sacred.

"A poet, like a glassblower, can create a wild celebration or a revealing whisper with the breath.

"Poems navigate the outlands of the mind to cross the abyss to the outlands of the heart, where reason has reasons it cannot understand.

"There are floating between worlds thousands of poems to dead children and loved ones who left before they could say good-bye. Words that bring closure.

"Medicine poetry opens the heart center, invites insight, calls on the light. Clearing the conduit to the heart, it addresses that part of us that endures.

"The medicinal qualities of poetry offer hidden healings."

Kuan Yin said your work is to bring that hidden healing to the surface in the individual's own words.

There are words in us
that don't know how
to get to the surface.

Words hidden in our marrow
afraid to show themselves
concerned the world will end
if they are uttered.
Words that cross
the river of pain
that wish to tell the world
how much love is hidden
just below our fear.
And some of these words
sometimes find their way
to live among us
in the trust to hear them,
words that spin our compass
anger and loneliness redirected
by insight and forgiveness,
words like mercy and compassion,
words we never trusted to exist.
Words hide in the strangest places,
under stones, in clouds,
in a moment of a friend's kindness,
in a moment of your generosity;
in poems beginning their first line
climbing happily into the heart singing
how close the moon comes
when we trust the night.
Words even hide in other words.
Mercy hides in the hesitant pause,
questioning how much can be trusted

to the tongue, to the pen.
Invoking their true voice
rise to the surface
to sing their original song.

She said that such shamanic medicine retrieving the "hidden word" when an individual's heart is ripe is often best transmitted through the invocation of the heart, which brings intuition to the surface. Giving voice to what remains hidden in an unexpected upwelling that unblocks the passageways to the heart.

The right word at the right time is strong medicine. Such words are a blessing to those states of mind when alternatives to suffering seem very far away. Words that transmit grace, a glimpse of our tranquil underlying nature.

"They rest in our intention for the well-being of another. How powerful these medicine words when whispered in the ear of a dying person. Or those who may have momentarily forgotten the enormity of their spirit.

"The difference," she said, "between a turning word and a hidden word is how long it takes us to discover what has always been there."

There is a sudden word that can make us
throw our old baggage over our shoulder
and hit the road in search of our true treasure.
It may come sometimes counting our breaths
deep in some surprising stream, passing through
the labyrinth around the heart

worn smooth from trying, clearing
the undergrowth that leaves us
in love for no earthly reason.

Words that turn us toward liberation as did "beloved"
for the dying nun, "generosity" for the giver, "mercy" for a
haggard mother, "forgiveness" when the heart has turned
to stone, "remember" when we have forgotten, "loving-
kindness" when that is the furthest thing from our mind,
or "reconciliation" when two people with the same state
of mind say they "have nothing in common."

> Breathing in, "What is the word?
> Breathing out, "hidden in everything?"
> Each inhalation uncovers
> what lies hidden and unborn.
> Breathing in and out
> in the mad house or
> on the meditation cushion,
> to find a word
> sane enough to save us.

When Long Nu was asked how one might find Kuan
Yin, she answered,

Let this body be born. Allow awareness

to come to the level of sensation.

Feel the breath breathe itself.

Breathing in, breathing out.

Soften the belly with each mindful rising

and falling of the abdomen.

Let the breath breathe itself in soft belly.

No resistance, no holding anywhere.

Notice awareness as the light of knowing

in the mind and body.

The light recognizes consciousness.

Letting go into the silence of wordless sensations.

Nothing to hold to, nothing remains but the
  sacred

emptiness which exudes mercy.

Letting go is freedom from what we hold to.

Surrender is victory.

An unexpected loving-kindness arising.

I am standing there, pure awareness.

Chapter 18

SHAN TSAI

The Dragon King also sent to Kuan Yin his adopted son Shan Tsai, the youth who had braved the marketplace, to be her attendant. Sending the beloved boy who longed for the teachings after having been saved from the fetid streets of a plague-ridden town to study in the bodhisattva's enlightening domain.

It was not as easy for Shan Tsai as it was for Long Nu who, upon coming into Kuan Yin's presence, had immediately become fulfilled.

Having viewed the courage and straightforwardness of the boy, Kuan Yin threw her shawl over him and recited to him the bodhisattva vow and began the teachings that such a commitment required: "Take the vow, commit yourself, without ambition, to live mindfully and heartfully for the benefit of another and all else as best you can. Merit is not something acquired by practice, but the liberation of your inborn qualities, the treasure of your original nature."

Kuan Yin's compassion tested the boy's resolve, unrolling before him the hardships of the path he vowed to follow. Could he take it? she asked, to which he bowed and touched his forehead to her feet. And when he rose, he was her student and attendant for this life and lives to come.

Sitting with the bright young man for some time, Kuan Yin spoke of the suffering and hopelessness he had gone through. She listened to the trembling in his out breath.

Tuning her breath to his, she lifted him out of his expectation and misery. As Kuan Yin breathed Shan Tsai's breath into her body, he saw the goal that was awaiting if he could keep his feet on the golden path. The way of mindfulness and mercy, the illumination at the center of awareness and the natural clarity of the heart.

No one had ever paid such close attention to him. Their breaths intertwining, she drew an *ahh* out of him with each exhalation. Knowing below his ordinary awareness that this *ahh* was a password to the heart, a cipher for the letting go that revealed compassion. Later she would demonstrate to him how softening the belly would become a trip-lever for letting go.

Experiencing the *ahh,* his teacher quoted another, Sri Nisargadatta Maharaj: "The mind creates the abyss, and the heart crosses it."

Joined in the tonal paradise of *ahh,* the peace that surpasses understanding descended on them.

Before taking birth, Shan Tsai's Buddha-nature sparked and whispered in his synapses.

All larval Buddhas wriggling precariously toward the Great Ocean. Some dead far up on the beach, some so close they'll know the way by heart next time around. And some, flopped, third eye–down in the luminescence at the edge, rising and falling ever so gently on the breath inside each wave.

In extended periods of meditation, vowing not to move, the senses opened deeper. He could hear and see clearly at a distance. Coming to the surface, gradually more accessible to compassion, the softening that triggers letting go into the body and opens the heart loosened the fetters that began falling away.

Watching how each moment, no matter how painful, or lit by delight, dissolved into the next, he experienced himself not so much as a thing, a noun, as a process, a verb. He was creation unfolding. No longer hypnotized by the monotony of thinking, his heart leapt incarnations. The mind turning back on itself saw its unfolding as an essentially impersonal process. The mind had a mind of its own. The heart illuminated the sun.

The healing he would share as one of the long-rumored "hidden bodhisattvas" leading, like Long Nu, to the conduit for many seeking answers only their true nature could provide.

Noticeably, Kuan Yin in some depictions is carrying a small basket in which two fish sons are swimming in the dragon's magnanimity, a perfect balance for the vase filled with the nectar of life in the other hand.

Entering realms of selfless service and care for all sentient beings, Shan Tsai and Long Nu cut through the fetters that drag us through hell, and, equally difficult to relinquish, heaven.

> Sometimes when we meditate
> there is nothing left of us
> but the breath,
> all that remains inseparable
> from all that is.
> Kuan Yin asks, "Who are you?"

This ghost-like "I" switching masks like a Chinese opera on the watery surface of consciousness is difficult to make out no matter how far we lean out of the boat or how soon we enter like Li Po the moon's reflection.

When the burning bush in the Old Testament is asked to identify itself, it attests, "I am that I am." It says I am that to which "I am" refers. I am amness, the ground of being, the link to the eternal.

When I am even momentarily resonating with the *humm* of being, I know "I am that" that emits compassion. Delving deeper into the mystical union I had hoped to achieve before her disappearance, she whispers in my heart saying:

"In order for the lizard to evolve into the bird, to change from cold-blooded to warm, able to dream and fly and sing, something that preexisted their birth just kept on going. The origin of song tells us that evolution is enlightenment. Who we really are, the heart of our true nature, is found beneath levels of consciousness and layers of conditioning as the song dries our wings.

"Indeed, until that first bird had that first dream of no longer being a lizard, the sacred never occurred to us."

After the teaching, Shan Tsai wrote:

We walk through half our life
As if it were a fever dream

Barely touching the ground,

Our eyes half-open
Our heart half-closed.

Not half knowing who we are
We watch the ghost of us drift
From room to room
Through friends and lovers
Never quite as real as advertised.

Not saying half we mean
Or meaning half we say
We dream ourselves
From birth to birth
Seeking some true self.

Until the fever breaks
And the heart cannot abide
A moment longer
As the rest of us awakens,
Summoned from the dream,
Not half-caring for anything but love.

Many people who have been drawn to Kuan Yin have
eventually taken her as their spirit guide, their *yiddam*, a
Tibetan term that designates an ever-present counselor,
an otherworldly personal deity. Discovering the original
seed of compassion within those who have protected and
nurtured mercy's precious growth through daily spiritual
practice. It takes effort to become effortless. In cultivating
her qualities of mercy, loving-kindness, and readiness to
serve, Shan Tsai's and Long Nu's lives mirror Kuan Yin's
presence in their hearts.

Playing the edge of our ancient conditioning, they surrender daily into their original Buddha-nature. Following
the trails intuition leaves across the cerebellum, they enter
into the heart-brain, the big Mind's natural outpouring
of loving-kindness where I and other merge into One.
Where compassion and care for others' well-being is an
immediate response.

Seeking to overcome the hindrances to the heart, our
selfishness and self-pity, fear and laziness, we become the
flowering tree that prospers from the well-cultivated seed

to become like the world-sheltering compassion of Kuan Yin.

Because of her total absorption in compassion, she became the formless Buddha of the present. This undifferentiated compassion allowed her to hold the suffering of the world in her boundless heart. As the Dalai Lama said, "No attachment, no compassion."

As compassion's Avalokiteshvara, she offered the great teaching that emptiness is the realization of form, form the participation of emptiness. Self-existent love.

"Somewhere in us is buried treasure."

There are blessings that arise in spiritual practice that seem too good to be true. But seeing there is nothing you know that you couldn't know at a deeper level, you go even beyond your training to discover aspects of yourself too beautiful for words.

Sometimes the heart opens spontaneously. There are earthquakes in the skull that rattle our knowing and knock all our trophies off their shelves. A sharp pain may flash across the side of the head. It says, "Sit up straight. What you were born for is coming!"

The tectonic plates in the skull shifting. Lightning in the temporal lobes. Angels to say the least and the simple clarity that reveals the floating worlds. Momentarily comprehending the nature of being, the mind becomes preternaturally patient.

An upwelling of the spirit finds us halfway up Jacob's ladder. A true word, a seismic word, has opened the top of the head, revealing a caldera that exposes strata after strata of consciousness. A rare ecological niche flourished with devas and the spirits of mendicants still following the subtle path. It is our primal song's origins, the origin of origins, which reveals a verdant valley whose bottomland is pure amness, the universal ground of being.

The only metaphor for this spiritual upwelling, this deeper awakening, is the snake shedding its skin to give it room to grow. As the heart expands, it finds itself in a greater body acting for the benefit of a larger world.

Chapter 19

REFLECTION ON THE MOTHER OF MERCY

Don't be embarrassed by your sorrow.

Let it sink into your heart and be swaddled in
mercy.

Loving-kindness flows through the grief point
directly into the heart.

The body fills with warmth.

Buddha said, "You could look the whole world
over and never find anyone more deserving of
love than yourself."

Mercy changes the game.

Our sorrow believes we deserve to suffer. Have
mercy on this stranger in you. Let this stranger
be reborn in a merciful consciousness.

How often might we consider death before we

    permit ourselves the life of the heart.

Let her loving-kindness open the fist around your

    heart.

The Mother of Mercy prays to free us from our

    image

of the perfection to which so much suffering

    clings.

When in the shadowy mind we imagine our-

    selves imperfectly,

praying to be freed by enlightenment, she refines

    our prayers.

Putting her arms around us

she bids us put our head on her shoulder

whispering, don't you know

with all your fear and anger

all you are fit for is love.

May all beings be free of suffering. May all beings

    be at peace.

Chapter 20

FORGIVENESS

Beginning to direct feelings of care and kindness to our loved ones and friends, and gradually expanding that circle to include those we do not even know. Bringing them to mind and directing toward them wishes for their well-being. Perhaps even using the traditional phrase, "May you be free from suffering, may you be at peace."

See how expanding this concern for others makes more room in your heart for you as well. Calling yourself by your first name, say, "May I be free of difficulty, may I be at peace."

Some days in a life of compassion and loving-kindness are gratefully dedicated to learning to keep our heart open even to our heart being closed. I know some remarkable people, even some who are considered great human beings, but I have never known anyone whose heart is open all the time. Even the Dalai Lama speaks of anger arising and of saying things that, much to his chagrin, can never be taken back. Forgiveness of oneself and others is a means of staying present rather than lost in remorse over past unskillful moments. Forgiveness works miracles.

Forgiveness Meditation

Bring to mind a person with whom you feel distance.

And, just as an experiment in truth, invite this person whom you feel has done you wrong into your heart for a moment. Imagine his presence, see him standing there, and note closely what you feel in his proximity. What happens when you turn toward, instead of away from, that person with whom you have unfinished business?

Notice the feelings that come up and how they inhibit your ability to turn the tide: fear, judgment, guilt, anger. Let these feelings come and go.

Now, in your mind, face this person and tell him that you forgive him. "I forgive you for whatever you may have done in the past that caused me pain—through your words, through your actions, even through your thoughts. However you caused me pain, intentionally or unintentionally, I forgive you."

Notice how just the heart speech of "I forgive you" to that person, even if it does not yet have much momentum, nonetheless softens the defenses, as it at least contemplates the possibility of forgiveness.

How does it feel when you begin to forgive others so as to have more room for yourself in your heart?

Have mercy on yourself by having mercy on others. Forgive them. Allow them to be touched by the possibility of your forgiveness. Let them into your heart. Forgive them for the moments in which their hearts could not yet see. Have mercy on yourself—forgive them.

It's so painful to put someone out of our heart. It deadens so many parts of us.

Forgive just as you wish to be forgiven. Forgive just as you perhaps wish someone who has put you out of her heart to let you back in. In your heart speech, you might say to her, "I ask for your forgiveness for whatever I may have done that caused you pain, intentionally or unintentionally. Whatever I may have said or done that caused you pain, I ask that you forgive me."

And, just as a continuation of this experiment in healing, allow yourself to be invited back into her heart and to feel her mercy. Allow yourself to be forgiven. Let yourself be touched by the possibility of her forgiveness. In your heart, send her gratitude and be open to her forgiveness.

Then, turning toward yourself in your heart, say, "I forgive you" to yourself. At first you might say this with a difficulty that defies the heart of mercy, but say it again: "I forgive you."

How long can you stand this self-judgment, this fear of yourself? What happens when you forgive yourself?

If your mind, in mercilessness, says that it's self-indulgent to forgive oneself, recognize this unkind, unhealed mind that's so angry and so pained.

Let it in. Breathe that forgiveness through the grief point directly into the touch point of the heart. Each breath draws forgiveness from the well of your deepest nature.

Turning toward yourself with forgiveness in your heart, call yourself by your own first name and say, "I forgive you" to yourself and feel your heart filling with mercy.

We are part of the plight and healing of all human-kind. Just as we wish to be free, so do all beings. Let your concern for others' well-being radiate outward to all who also want only to be free from pain.

And in your heart-speech, say to those in your life, in your memory, "May you be free from suffering. May you be at peace."

Let your mercy, let your forgiveness, and your heart's sweet success at its willingness to be forgiven, fill the mind and the world with loving-kindness.

Let this sense of merciful connection with yourself keep expanding until the whole world floats like a bubble in the ocean of compassion that is your heart. Let your mercy, your forgiveness, your loving-kindness embrace this suffering planet.

And listen in your heart to the voice of innumerable hearts rising in chorus: "May all beings everywhere be free from suffering. May all beings be at peace."

Many people may notice they have taken the same person for both aspects of the forgiveness practice: forgiving someone and alternately asking him for forgiveness as well.

Stella, a pained example of conflicting feelings of resentment and duty, said of attending to her once-abusive dying father, "I didn't do something for my dad that I should have when he was dying. I wasn't there with him. I should have been there. He died alone."

We are so conditioned to feel guilty that we are often loath to admit any anger toward the person we feel we have let down. We cannot expect the mind to be rational under such circumstances. Having hurt someone whom we feel hurt us, the vertigo of blame and shame spins out. We try to bury what we consider an aberration, but the difficulty in forgiving oneself persists. Not realizing, odd as it sounds, that it is not until we forgive the other person that we will be able to forgive ourselves.

It may be that you have to forgive the person you most think you want forgiveness from. When you do that, you will then be able to turn openhearted toward yourself.

MAY ALL BEINGS BE FREE OF THE HINDRANCES
TO COMPASSION

MAY ALL BEINGS LISTEN WITH THE EAR OF MERCY

Chapter 21

THE GRADUAL
MAITREYA

There is an old hardworking spiritual that says, "People get ready, there's a train a-comin'," which may now refer to the vehicle by which we return to our Original Heart. Maitreya, who may be the old Chinese beggar-monk Pu Tai, whose name means "harmonious with this," rumored to be the heart of the coming era, is on the way back, with his sack full of enlightened gifts for the children. The Buddha who cannot stop laughing at the absurdity of things is riding this way like a rodeo cowboy on Kuan Yin's dragon.

Maitreya, the next wave of wisdom and compassion, the formless Buddha, has been entering for some time. Potentiating the teachings in loving-kindness and the power to clear the path with a merciful awareness.

Maitreya, a selflessness deep in the heart of Pu Tai, crossed the great waters disguised as an acceptable myth, or sometimes a Japanese wooden trinket hands akimbo to the heavens, about a century ago to inspire dreams that heal, and healings.

Recognizing the need to transmit an expanded heart dharma, perhaps as silently as Gautama's transmission to Kassapa in a flower. The spirit of Maitreya knows it must cultivate the season of the heart in a manner that does not startle the fear of change experienced even by those leaving hell. Smuggling his altruistic spirit into traditional children's stories or disguised as a fat little Buddha curio throwing his hands to the heavens in dusty bric-a-brac Chinatown shops. Japanese Ho Tai having jumped the straits now comes to heal America, entering the home as a forgotten souvenir.

Mountains and rivers know Pu Tai Maitreya best. Living on the east wall of old temples, remembered most in holy places, biding his time, perhaps forgotten in the back of a cluttered drawer alongside some slim goddess, talismans of our innate enormity.

Maitreya is the increasing relationship with our true nature through translations of Buddhism and Hindu wisdom for almost two hundred years. The poet and journalist Rick Fields told of what seems to be Maitreya's swan settling onto the great waters of the West. Rick's history of the inception of Buddhism in America cracking the egg and making our omelet. Maitreya says, "Breakfast is served!" And just for balance in this nineteenth-century outpouring, beside our morning paper was the Upanishads.

Maitreya returns as a tendency to balance disharmony. A turning of the head toward the heart. A kindness reminding us to soften our belly and open our heart to serve others and keep the faith; and let loose the joy-inducing smile or at least the half smile, which Thich Nhat Hanh recommends.

Maitreya is all the hidden bodhisattvas and bodhisattvas-in-training, right-minded adherents committed to the well-being of others. Those attempting to maintain an intention to serve the difficulties the path has brought into view. It includes of course those committed to the well-being of others who have never heard of the bodhisattva vow.

It is not easy to keep the heart open in another's hell. The will to serve can deplete even the most wholehearted among us: the knotted therapists and weeping priests of every faith; the spiritual teachers who listen for a way through the raw contents of our struggling minds; the "godsent" passersby in the supermarket who hold palm-to-palm the depressed as they deconstruct in the midst of the aisle, saying they don't know how to shop for just one. The trusted neighbor, the kind stranger, and all those kindly bent to ease the pain of a sometimes wretched world.

The peacekeepers, the heartful teachers, the earth protectors, the gardeners of Buddha-nature, working elbow by elbow serving the broken, ill-fated, and poverty-stricken in shelters, prisons, and hospitals. Those undercover angels who openhandedly offer whatever spiritual strength is available; loosening finger by finger the fist of fear that grasps the heart. The wounded menders of the wounded who offer hidden words that remind the heart during the day and the turning words that direct us in our dreams.

The highest bodhisattvas like Kuan Yin are beingness constellated in form as a courtesy to those whose hand is extended. They untie entanglements, align the wobbly orbits of errant stars, invoke the ultimate empathy inseparable from unconditional love.

Maitreya comes now as the new science, the science of brain and mind. The newest research that compares electromagnetic imaging (similar to encephalographs) of the workings of the cerebral brain-mind to the workings of the cerebral brain, that does our thinking for us and insists it is the only reality, compared to the apparently several times most distinct emanations of the heart center that observes it all without judgment. The cerebral cortex exhorts us to keep our eyes on the job at hand while the emanations of the heart suggest we be mindful or lose the healing we took birth for.

The cerebral mind identified with its conditioning, gain and loss; and the ongoing construction of the self-image is the mostly self-concerned small self. It navigates by aversion to pain-fear and attraction to pleasure, appointment, and disappointment. Individualistic, isolated. More romantic than altruistic.

The heart-brain, the universal Self, has a wider perspective. It includes others in pain as well, and the power to observe with clear compassion the nature of the mechanical mind. Taking pain as a teaching in compassion, it embodies the bodhisattva vow to work on oneself as a responsibility to all sentient beings, cultivating a merciful awareness, loving-kindness, generosity, forgiveness, and gratitude; exploring our potential for being increasingly loving. When the heart-mind embraces the mechanical cerebral, allowing it to see beyond itself, some discover that the unconditioned mind is indistinguishable from unconditional love.

Kuan Yin's emissary, Tian, painted Maitreya as a splash of form, a wandering monk, an alms-giving bag slung over his left shoulder, smiling like later Buddhas would. A hidden teaching that breaks sorrow in his gift-giving tote, mercy and the end of madness, the wound-healing gem of loving-kindness and kind attention. Joy in the stillness between thoughts. His image is the true illusion revealed to the hidden eye: a smoky waterfall clothes him, a dark sash ties heaven to earth. His head kindly tilted. Eyes like specks of coal compressed under the weight of ten thousand extinctions and reappearances. Like Kuan Yin the same different Buddha.

Traditional painters did not dare put their red seal on such a painting; they did not want to presume or miss a hidden word.

Having met before time, Kuan Yin snuck an additional talisman for sorrowful children in the Gradual Maitreya's gift-bestowing sack. In Pu Tai's great medicine bag of renewal, besides Kuan Yin's medicine tears, was also Long Nu's pearl of great luminescence, and Tibetan Tara's blessing of absolute stillness. And from Miao Shan a reminder of service to all, from a world of diminishing wildings, to the beds of dying clergy, bestowing the bodhisattva vow.

To repay her gratitude, Pu Tai purloined the peaches of immortality, which he waited three thousand years to ripen by the celestial tree of life, so that Kuan Yin might take them with her and live forever to be present each time Maitreya returned with the light by which Kuan Yin may be most easily recognized.

Becoming Kuan Yin

Chapter 22

DEVOTION TO COMPASSION

Sometimes devotion has nowhere to go but in. We watch our resistance to taking ourselves into our whole heart, to calling ourselves by our true name, to turning to ourselves and bowing to the Beloved.

The tendency toward devotion is a natural outpouring of our underlying tendency to love. The tendency toward devotion, which can be greater than any particular object of devotion, can go unsatisfied until we find our "place" in the world, our love, our life practice.

Devotion includes devotion to all things. To mate, family, friends; indeed, to all sentient beings, to nature itself, to the earth, and to all beings on every level of existence seen and unseen.

Devotion bids us come to the edge of the flat world and look past the predictable to the wild lands that lie beyond the rational mind, entering realms only the trust that love engenders might take us through.

When being loving becomes even more important than being loved, true devotion is experienced. A loving that does not depend on getting what we want but on offering what the world and our hearts cry out for.

Devoted to self-discovery, to that which inquires into its own nature, to uncovering the Self in self, sensed on a previously unrecognized path.

Devotion is surrender. Surrender begins in the belly and rises to the heart. Every once in a while a prayer or insight or a conscious breath carries it up through the crown of the skull.

Softening the belly, freeing one breath after the other, they rise through the heart, and foregoing heaven continue upward past the flowering pastures behind the brow, to ascend to whatever comes next. Each breath filled with the kindness we most trust. Each breath breathed as though it were our last. Each breath breathed for the benefit of all sentient beings.

Making connection with our essential nature expanding somewhere deep within us, there is a greater vulnerability to the truth in the sacred heart, the winged heart, the radiant heart, the Torah heart, the Gita heart, the Psalms, the original song, as our feet lift from the mount, as we sit in the desert bent forty days by the rock, as we surrender even hope beneath the bo tree so that nothing obscures the sacred fire, the heart into which other hearts dissolve.

Chapter 23

LOST AND FOUND

After months of sitting each night at Kuan Yin's feet to transcribe her book, one morning upon waking, eager to finish the transmission of the preceding night, my page was blank. My mind recalled nothing. Kuan Yin's direct transmission was nowhere to be found. She was nowhere to be found. To my dismay, there wasn't a single word to be written. Turning to look at a small bronze Kuan Yin on the nightstand beside me, there was just a lump of melted metal. Our connection seemed broken!

From her endless compassion, she offered me her absence as a teaching to go further. To discard some idea of her as separate, no longer defined by form but as active emptiness.

She called me to overcome my addiction to the pleasure of her company and sink into the featureless depths of compassion itself. To bow to the revealed nature of myself; that Pure Land between the eyes, the primordial wisdom behind the brow. Her absence was the dearest of her encouragements to find what was real.

The image that had been an object of encouragement and gratitude became, in my attachment to it, an object lesson in the cause of suffering and the end of suffering. It was the pain that ends pain. Clearly it was not Kuan Yin who was somehow causing me distress but a remnant will to own God, to hold satisfaction close.

I remembered one of Kuan Yin's old devotees saying, "It is to draw us closer that she sustains her playful illusion that she is separate from us."

Though we alert ourselves to the pain of desire we can't dismiss the heart's longing to know its true self. In the fulfillment of temporal desire, there is a moment of cessation when, experiencing that state of mind of "satisfaction" we are addicted to, as gratification occurs, desire for an instant ceases and we get a glimpse of the light of the underlying Great Satisfaction. Habitual wanting and needing part like the Red Sea, and we see what lies beyond. The Great Satisfaction shining through, whether we call it completely empty or completely full, God or dharma, bliss or boundless thankfulness.

Kuan Yin's longing to free "those who cannot yet see," Jesus' and Mary's hopefulness, Buddha's regret that he could not reach everyone, keeps the very human bodhisattva in us active on this terrible/wonderful plain. Gandhi encouraged that his God was by his side when the bullets struck. Such pure longing, made of fire and joy, faces us rightly.

The heart has a life of its own. Sometimes its momentum carries us beyond our understanding and waits patiently for us to catch up. We find ourselves loving for no reason whatsoever. We are simply in love, and all that comes close we are "in love" with. Pascal said the heart has reasons the mind cannot understand. To paraphrase what Thomas Merton said, "Union (heart yoga) is learned when prayer has become impossible and the heart has turned to stone." When no obstruction, in form or concept, confines the unlimited clarity of a merciful consciousness, we are in the heart of the matter. Love is the highest form of acceptance, fear the resistance of nonacceptance. Love, one might say, is heaven; but heaven without compassion is hell.

Kuan Yin's presence is the abode of compassion in which we live; the deep satisfaction of generosity and gratitude, loving-kindness and sympathetic joy, forgiveness, patience, mercy, and a lifetime commitment to self-discovery and the well-being of others.

ABOUT THE AUTHOR

Stephen Levine and his wife and spiritual partner Ondrea have been teaching Buddhist meditation practices to dharma students, prisoners, and the ill for more than thirty years. Their talks and interviews on *Levinetalks.com* have been widely respected, and their skillful means adopted in various hospices, hospitals, and universities. Stephen's guided meditations have been particularly useful to the dying and grieving as well as for the uncovering of hidden healings.

Stephen's books have been translated into eighteen languages. They are: *A Gradual Awakening, Who Dies: An Investigation of Conscious Living and Conscious Dying, Meetings at the Edge: Dialogues with the Grieving and Dying, Healing into Life and Death, Guided Meditations: Investigations and Healings, Embracing the Beloved: Relationship as a Path of Awakening* (with Ondrea), *Unattended Sorrow: Recovering from Loss and Reviving the Heart, Turning Toward the Mystery: A Seeker's Journey, A Year to Live: How to Live This Year as if It Were Your Last,* and *In the Time of the Smiling Buddhas: Opening the Eye of Beauty of a Sung Dynasty Landscape Painter.*

Visit him at *www.levinetalks.com.*

TO OUR READERS